Self-Disclosure

SAGE SERIES ON CLOSE RELATIONSHIPS

Series Editors
Clyde Hendrick, Ph.D., and
Susan S. Hendrick, Ph.D.

Self-Disclosure

Valerian J. Derlega,
Sandra Metts,
Sandra Petronio,
Stephen T. Margulis

Sage
Series
on Close
Relationships

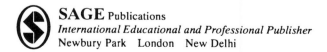

SAGE Publications
International Educational and Professional Publisher
Newbury Park   London   New Delhi

2710 6113

For information address:

SAGE Publications, Inc.
2455 Teller Road
Newbury Park, California 91320

SAGE Publications Ltd.
6 Bonhill Street
London EC2A 4PU
United Kingdom

SAGE Publications India Pvt. Ltd.
M-32 Market
Greater Kailash I
New Delhi 110 048 India

Printed in the United States of America

Library of Congress Cataloging-in-Publication Data

Main entry under title:

Self-disclosure / Valerian J. Derlega. . . [et al.].
      p. cm. —(Sage series on close relationships)
  Includes bibliographical references and index.
  ISBN 0-8039-3954-X —ISBN 0-8039-3955-8 (pb)
  1. Self-disclosure. 2. Interpersonal relations. I. Derlega,
Valerian J II. Series.
BF697.5.S427S43 1993
158'.2—dc20   92-42034

93 94 95 96 10 9 8 7 6 5 4 3 2 1

Sage Production Editor: Diane S. Foster

Contents

Series Editors' Introduction

When we first began our work on love attitudes more than a decade ago, we did not know what to call our research area. In some ways it represented an extension of earlier work in interpersonal attraction. Most of our scholarly models were psychologists (though sociologists had long been deeply involved in the areas of courtship and marriage), yet we sometimes felt as if our work had no professional "home." That has all changed. Our research not only has a home, but it also has an extended family, and the family is composed of relationship researchers. During the past decade the discipline of close relationships (also called personal relationships and intimate relationships) has emerged, developed, and flourished.

Two aspects of close relationships research should be noted. The first is its rapid growth, resulting in numerous books, journals, handbooks, book series, and professional organizations. As fast as the field grows, the demand for even more research and knowledge seems to be ever increasing. Questions about close, personal relationships still far exceed answers. The second noteworthy aspect of the new discipline of closer relationships is its interdisciplinary nature. The field owes its vitality to scholars from communi- cations, family studies and human development, psychology (clinical, counseling, developmental, social), and sociology, as well as other disciplines such as nursing and social work. It is this interdisciplinary wellspring that gives close relationships research its diversity and richness, qualities that we hope to achieve in the current series.

The **Sage Series on Close Relationships** is designed to acquaint diverse readers with the most up-to-date information about various topics in close relationships theory and research. Each volume in the series covers a particular topic or theme in one area of close relationships. Each book reviews the particular topic area, describes contemporary research in the area (including the authors' own work, where appropriate), and offers some suggestions for interesting research questions and/or real-world applications related to the topic. The volumes are designed to be appropriate for students and professionals in communication, family studies, psychology, sociology, and social work, among others. A basic assumption of the series is that the broad panorama of close relationships can best be portrayed by authors from multiple disciplines so that the series cannot be "captured" by any single disciplinary bias.

The current volume, *Self-Disclosure*, places self-disclosure squarely in the center of the interpersonal communication that can make or break an intimate relationship. Val Derlega, Sandra Metts, Sandra Petronio, and Stephen Margulis are creative and very timely as they discuss disclosure in the context of relationship transformation, as a vehicle for displaying gender similarities and differences, and as a means of psychological (and perhaps physical) healing. This volume offers a clear, fresh articulation of self-disclosure as a fundamental ingredient of human communication.

CLYDE HENDRICK
SUSAN S. HENDRICK
SERIES EDITORS

Preface

This book focuses on the role of self-disclosure in close relation-ships. We show how individuals negotiate with their relation-ship partners: what, when, where, and how they communicate personal feelings and thoughts about themselves and their relation-ship with one another. Although self-disclosure is not equivalent to and does not define the level of intimacy of a relationship, it is one major factor in the development, maintenance, and deterioration of a relationship. Conversely the level of closeness between relation-ship partners (whether the individuals are acquaintances, friends, lovers, or relatives) affects the meaning and impact of disclosure.

We focus on four major themes, illustrating how self-disclosure operates in relationships and how relationship partners interact with one another. The themes emphasize (a) how close relationships and self-disclosure are *mutually transformative*, where self-disclosure and relationships mutually interact to affect one another; (b) how *subcultural differences* between males and females influence self-disclosure in relationships; (c) how the vulnerability and risk associated with disclosing personal information leads relationship partners to be concerned about *privacy regulation;* and (d) how *stress-reducing disclosure,* associated with the willingness to talk about stressful events, provides both a means of coping with unpleasant life events and an access to social support.

We hope that coverage of these major themes and other self-disclosure issues will be useful to students, researchers, and practitioners interested in studying close relationships. In addition, we have included, in Chapters 2, 3, 4, and 5, questionnaire materials to illustrate how data might be collected on various topics related to self-disclosure research.

In preparing this book, we wish to acknowledge the support of the editors of the Sage Series on Close Relationships—Clyde Hendrick and Susan Hendrick. We owe Clyde and Susan many thanks for their patience and advice. We extend gratitude to colleagues in the field of close relationships who made available preprints and reprints of their work. Special thanks also are extended to those who gave us permission to use the copyrighted materials that appear in the book.

One of the many pleasures in writing this book has been the opportunity for the authors, trained in related but distinct disciplines, to collaborate together. Val Derlega and Steve Margulis were trained as social psychologists, and Sandra Metts and Sandra Petronio were trained as communication researchers. It is a source of considerable satisfaction for us to participate in the continuing dialogue among professionals in communications, social psychology, and family relations who study close relationships.

Finally we note with sadness the untimely death of John H. Berg (May 5, 1952 - May 20, 1991), who died from complications associated with multiple sclerosis. John was a prominent contributor to research and theory on self-disclosure in close relationships. John had planned to collaborate with us in writing this book. We dedicate the book to him.

1

Self-Disclosure:
A Useful Behavior for Studying
Close Relationships

Self-disclosure, loosely defined as what individuals verbally reveal about themselves to others (including thoughts, feelings, and experiences), plays a major role in close relationships. Imagine that you have just been introduced to someone at a party. What do you say to one another? You may talk about the music or the people at the party. You are not yet willing to self-disclose. But if you discover that this person has observations or opinions that are similar to your own or if you are attracted for other reasons, you may begin to tell this person things about yourself (what you are taking at school or where you come from) and to ask him or her questions. Soon you know something about your new acquaintance and he or she knows something about you. You have begun to self-disclose to one another.

It is hard to imagine how a relationship might get started without such self-disclosure. If you like this person, you will want to know more about him or her, and you will, in turn, be willing to share more information about yourself. You will begin to talk about attitudes, feelings, and personal experiences; in brief, you will begin to disclose more personal information. If your new friend likes you, he or she also will disclose personal information. Self-disclosure is an important component of the development of a close relationship.

In addition to getting to know one another through self-disclosure, telling someone something truly personal about yourself conveys a kind of information beyond the content of the disclosure. It says that you trust that person to respond appropriately to the revealed information and, in some cases, to keep that information between the two of you. When we receive very personal disclosures from another, we may feel closer to that person because we know he or she trusts us and values our response.

A casual reading of early work on self-disclosure in close relationships, including incremental exchange theory (Levinger & Snoek, 1972), social penetration theory (Altman & Taylor, 1973), and the "humanistic" psychology of Sidney Jourard (1971b) and Carl Rogers (1970), might suggest that self-disclosure is synonymous with a close relationship. Self-disclosure can contribute to developing a close relationship (for instance, one person's disclosure may be used by the other person to draw inferences about whether the two might get along), and self-disclosure may contribute to relationship maintenance (partners may listen carefully to one another's complaints about the relationship instead of trying to "read" the other's mind). Self-disclosure between individuals, however, is not equivalent to having a close relationship. Think of the concept of "love at first sight." Sometimes we feel very close to a person whom we hardly know. True, in time we may learn a lot about that person, but our initial feelings of involvement need not depend on intimate self-disclosures. Also, in an established close relationship the partners may choose not to reveal certain personal information to one another. In close relationships couples negotiate what they will talk about, as well as what they will not talk about. Also, individuals may have different techniques (other than disclosure) for finding out about another person with whom they potentially might want to be involved in a relationship (Baxter & Wilmot, 1984) and may have many channels for conveying information about themselves without talking directly about their feelings and thoughts (Patterson, 1990).

ᐛ A Functional Analysis of Self-Disclosure

Self-disclosure may serve different functions or goals in a relationship (Archer, 1987; Derlega & Grzelak, 1979; Miller & Read, 1987). We already have mentioned the goal of relationship development. Another purpose of self-disclosure is social validation, getting feedback from others about our thoughts or feelings or getting help with problems in our lives; or we may use self-disclosure for social control, selectively presenting information about ourselves to create a good impression.

Individuals may consider their own, as well as their partner's, interests in deciding whether to divulge or be the recipient for certain information during a social interaction. But self-disclosure also may be used to satisfy personal goals that are antithetical to the needs of the other person. For example, consider the norm of reciprocity for self-disclosure. When one person divulges something personal, it is expected that the disclosure recipient will tell something personal in return or will behave in a way that communicates interest in and/ or understanding of what was said (Berg, 1987; Berg & Archer, 1980; Chaikin & Derlega, 1974). Most of us have had the experience of getting into a conversation with someone who begins to tell us very personal things about him- or herself. If we are not interested in developing a relationship with this person, we may feel uncomfortable. Perhaps without being aware of it, we are responding to the unspoken assumption that we too will divulge personal information when we really do not want to.

It is important to note that, in successful relationships, partners negotiate what they talk about with one another (e.g., Coupland, Coupland, Giles, & Wieman, 1988), and decisions about self-disclosure are not made in isolation by individuals. Self-disclosure occurs as part of ongoing social interactions between relationship partners, and interactants must determine jointly what, when, where, and how they will communicate with one another, including whether to disclose private feelings about themselves individually or about their relationship with one another. Thus what individuals divulge is influenced by the context provided by the ongoing conversation, events that are happening to the relationship partners (past, present, and anticipated future), as well as by the feelings that the partners have for their relationship. Individuals do not decide by themselves what to talk about without considering the social context provided by the relationship between the interaction partners. As Holtgraves (1990) perceptively wrote: "[It] is misleading to consider self-disclosure as an individual phenomenon. Rather, the emphasis is on the joint contributions of the interactants through the give and take of a conversation. In the end, both what is disclosed, and its significance, are to be viewed as a collective, emergent phenomenon" (p. 196).

Decisions that persons make about self-disclosure have consequences not only for the individual partners in a relationship but also for the relationship itself. Individuals may select and package their disclosure messages with the goal of creating a certain desired impression or self-presentation. However, particularly in a close relationship in which individuals have a high investment and commitment, individuals also may negotiate what to talk about and in what manner. Both the discloser and the disclosure recipient may avoid talking about certain topics that might prove too threatening to them (e.g., a husband and wife might avoid talking about any negative feelings they have for one another because they are afraid of what might happen next, or a wife, recognizing that her unemployed husband is embarrassed about not working, may not ask him how his job hunting went that day). To protect one another, relationship partners also may encourage and accept disclosure messages that are stated "indirectly" instead of "directly" (Holtgraves, 1990; Petronio, 1991). For instance, if your spouse or roommate usually has a bad day at work, it might be enough if he or she says with a facetious tone of voice, "It was just another day at the office."

⮞ The Content of Self-Disclosure

What is the content of self-disclosure? Self-disclosure messages usually refer to *descriptive self-disclosures*—that is, information and facts about oneself that might be more or less personal, such as "My drinking habits," "Details about my sex life," or "I have four brothers and sisters"—and *evaluative self-disclosures*—that is, expressions of personal feelings, opinions, and judgments, such as "I am embarrassed to tell you what I feel," "I love you," or "I *hate* broccoli" (Morton, 1976, 1978). Many other dimensions of self-disclosure could be enumerated (see descriptions by Chelune, Skiffington, & Williams, 1981; Coupland et al., 1988; Derlega & Grzelak, 1979; Holtgraves, 1990), including the positivity-negativity of the information divulged, the voluntariness of information disclosed, the reward value that the information provides for the discloser or the listener, the informativeness of the disclosure message (how much information is provided about the causes underlying the discloser's behavior), and the reasons or attributions for the disclosing behavior itself.

Given this book's attention to self-disclosure in close relationships, it is also useful to make a distinction between *personal self-disclosure* (disclosure about oneself) and *relational self-disclosure* (disclosure that has as its referent one's relationship with another person or one's interactions with others). (See Baxter, 1987; Chelune, Robinson, & Kommor, 1984; and McAdams, 1984, for further discussion of this distinction.) Relational self-disclosure potentially has a role in relationship maintenance if partners can benefit from talking with one another about the state of their relationship and how they are communicating and interacting with one another (see Waring, 1987).

Our analysis of self-disclosure focuses on *verbal* messages that individuals disclose to one another and how persons react to being recipients of this information. It is also possible for individuals to divulge their feelings by a tone of voice, a hand gesture, or other nonverbal channels of communication. We deliberately have limited our analysis of self-disclosure to the verbal exchange of messages in order to make our task manageable. It is theoretically important, however, to consider how verbal and nonverbal behavior may operate together in self-disclosure, and important contributions have been made in this direction (e.g., Altman & Taylor, 1973; Argyle & Dean, 1965; Montgomery, 1981, 1984; Patterson, 1990).

≥ Overview of Chapters

Our goal in this book is to illustrate the usefulness of self-disclosure in understanding what happens in close relationships. Each of the following chapters emphasizes a major theme that organizes the literature in a particular area of self-disclosure research.

In Chapter 2 we describe how self-disclosure influences and is influenced by a developing close relationship. We suggest how close relationships and self-disclosure are *mutually transformative*, meaning that they continually interact to influence one another as a relationship evolves. Thus self-disclosure can affect the meaning and intensity of a relationship, while the nature of a relationship also can affect reactions to self-disclosure. We discuss transformation agents that influence the connections between self-disclosure and relationship development.

In Chapter 3 we examine the research on the effects of gender for self-disclosure in close relationships. We suggest that *subcultural differences between males and females* may influence gender-related decisions about self-disclosure. Males and females who are raised in North American culture (emphasis on white, Protestant, northern European background) may value different goals in close relationships, which, in turn, can influence their communicative behavior. The notion of subcultural differences between the sexes guides our review of research on what males and females talk about in same- and opposite-sex relationships and suggests how misunderstandings may occur between men and women.

In Chapter 4 we describe how relationship partners attempt to balance the competing needs to share personal information while at the same time preserving a sense of *privacy*. Because the disclosure of personal information may create risks (e.g., being rejected by the disclosure recipient or having the information divulged to third parties), individuals seek to maintain privacy by controlling the amount and kind of information they disclose, as well as by restricting the range of persons to whom sensitive information is revealed. We emphasize how decisions about self-disclosure and privacy regulation must be coordinated in successful relationships to avoid threats to the partners or to the relationship itself.

In Chapter 5 we examine *stress-reducing disclosure*—how self-disclosure may be useful in coping with stressful events and in obtaining social support. We review theory and research indicating a linkage between confiding/nonconfiding and health outcomes. The psychological benefits of self-disclosure in coping with stress may be due, in part, to self-disclosure itself. We also show how the social benefits of self-disclosure depend on reactions that others provide to the disclosure input.

In Chapter 6, the epilogue, we present a self-disclosure quiz to review the major topics discussed in the book. We conclude by noting that self-disclosure is an important focal point for studying and understanding close relationships. We hope that readers will find the book valuable and rewarding in this endeavor.

2

Developing Close Relationships

I only regret that everyone wants to deprive me of the journal, which is the only steadfast friend I have, the only one which makes my life bearable; because my happiness with human beings is so precarious, my confiding moods rare, and the least sign of non-interest is enough to silence me.

Anais Nin (June 1933)
(in Stuhlmann, 1966, p. 224)

Yes, there is no doubt that paper is patient and as I don't intend to show this cardboard-covered notebook . . . to anyone, unless I find a real friend, boy or girl, probably nobody cares. And now I come to the root of the matter, the reason for my diary: it is that I have no such real friend.

Anne Frank
(in Moffat & Painter, 1974, p. 15)

These two diary entries are elegant testimonies to the duality of self-disclosure: It can indeed be a frightening venture, opening the teller to rejection or indifference, but at the same time it can be confirmation of one's worth and one of the greatest rewards provided by intimate relationships. Perhaps, after a bad experience with self-disclosure, you have felt as Anais Nin that revealing something important to another person is a bit too risky for comfort, and you have avoided it for some period of time. You also may have recognized, as did Anne Frank, that a "real friend" is the one who cares about who you are and what you say.

Obviously part of the complexity of self-disclosure stems from the fact that the consequences of self-disclosure are in some ways independent of what the teller might intend. In this regard, self-disclosure can have multiple effects—some anticipated, some not. For this reason, when we talk about the role of self-disclosure in the development of close relationships, we cannot talk about a simple cause-and-effect association; that is, we cannot say that self-disclosure always causes a relationship to develop or that relationship development always causes self-disclosure. These two concepts are associated with each other in complicated ways.

The goal of this chapter is to illustrate how self-disclosure becomes part of the emerging context of a relationship. We explore how self-disclosure influences and is influenced by such ongoing processes as partners negotiating a relationship definition, attempting to meet their individual goals, attempting to fit comfortably within social and family networks, and so forth. As a way to represent the interacting nature of self-disclosure and relationship development, we offer the phrase "mutually transformative." To say that disclosure and relationships are mutually transformative means that sometimes self-disclosure changes the direction, definition, or intensity of a relationship, whereas sometimes the nature of the relationship changes the meaning or impact of self-disclosure. Because this is an important notion in understanding self-disclosure in close relationships, we explore it in more detail in the following section.

ஃ Self-Disclosure and Relationships Are Mutually Transformative

Bob and Kathy met during their senior year in college. Their attraction to each other was immediate and intense. In an effort to build the relationship on a foundation of trust, Kathy told Bob about her previous relationships. Bob commended her honesty and assured her that the present was all that mattered to him. Just before graduation, however, the stress of exams, papers, and job hunting took a toll on the relationship. One Saturday evening Kathy went dancing with some friends at a local bar. The next morning, Bob called to break off the relationship, saying that he should have known from the very beginning that Kathy could not be trusted.

To understand the phrase *mutually transformative*, it is necessary to consider for a moment that both self-disclosure and relationships are dynamic and subjective. They exist (are understood in a meaningful way) largely in our perceptions of them. For example, if a relative stranger tells you a good deal of personal information during a few intense conversations, you may feel that you have formed a special friendship. This is more likely to be your assessment when you too have disclosed personal information; after all, we assume that we would not disclose to a relative stranger in the way we would to a friend. On the other hand, if you do not like what this person tells you because it seems inappropriate to your initial view of the relationship as one of relative strangers, you are not likely to respond favorably to the disclosure, and your definition of the relationship will severely constrain any effect on relational change. By the same token, if you have disclosed a memory of failure or shame to a lover during an especially tender moment, only to have it brought up with derision during a period of relationship deterioration, you have experienced a transformation in disclosure interpretation, based on a change in the relationship. How could your partner have been so understanding at one point in time and then used your disclosure so callously during another?

Transformations occur because messages are always received into a matrix of expectations, perceptions, and understandings of relational rules that give meaning to messages and that also change in light of these meanings. If the message is disclosing, the receiver reacts not only to the information but also to what it seems to say about the relationship, the character and intentions of the sender, implications for future interactions, and so forth. In the previous example, if a relational partner uses intimate disclosure as a weapon to hurt his or her partner, it may well be that in his or her mind, the relationship rules somehow have changed to "allow" this usage to count as fair play. Of course, this change in the rules will be noted by his or her partner, and other areas of trust may become fair game. Lovers become adversaries, and self-disclosure becomes a weapon.

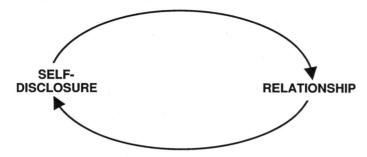

Figure 2.1. Mutual Transformation

In fact, even when self-disclosure of feelings might be meant positively (e.g., "I missed you last night"), it can be treated negatively by an angry partner (e.g., "Why? Do you need to be with me every moment?"). In short, self-disclosure messages transform the nature of the relationship, and the nature of the relationship transforms the meaning and consequences of the self-disclosure. This process is depicted in Figure 2.1.

Because the connection between disclosure and relationship change is *mutually transformative,* to understand how this process functions, we need a way to talk about relational change and a way to comprehend the mutual transformations between disclosure and relationships.

❧ A Model of Relational Development and Decline

To better understand how friendships or romantic relationships change, scholars such as Mark Knapp (1984) have proposed that relationships follow a life cycle through different stages of development. According to Knapp, these stages are characterized by certain patterns in behavior, feelings, thoughts, and communication. For example, in early stages, uncertainty is high and communication might be awkward, stylized, impersonal, and nonjudgmental. In later stages, uncertainty is low and communication might become smoother, more spontaneous, more personal, more judgmental, and tokens of affection might be exchanged.

In their "staircase model of relationship stages," Knapp and Vangelisti (1991) suggested that relationships move through two complementary processes: coming together and coming apart. In *coming together*, five stages represent the development of a relationship: initiating, experimenting, intensifying, integrating, and bonding. During *initiating*, relative strangers engage in small talk and role-appropriate behavior. During *experimenting*, they ask questions about preferences, activities, demographic information, and generally explore topics that might reveal similarities and common interests. Some degree of self-disclosure is likely at this stage, but not negative or highly personal disclosure. During *intensifying*, self-disclosure breadth and depth increases, and commitment is expressed verbally, sexually, and symbolically through exchanging keys, tokens, and so on. During *integrating*, self-disclosure continues to increase, the social network comes to see the pair as a couple, and the couple plans the future together and develops a joint identity. An engagement ring often is exchanged for romantic couples. *Bonding* is a stage marked by a public ritual, typically marriage (though business partners and friends also may have public rituals of commitment).

Knapp and Vangelisti (1991) also proposed five stages for the *coming apart* process that reflect disengagement from a relationship: differentiating, circumscribing, stagnating, avoiding, and terminating. During the *differentiating* stage, a couple begins to separate themselves psychologically from their joint identity and to present themselves to the social network as individuals. Differences rather than similarities are stressed. Joint property is split, and shared tokens are returned. During *circumscribing*, important topics are avoided, and discussions of the future are replaced by a focus on the present. During *stagnating*, physical and psychological distance is so pronounced that even conflict is unlikely. The couple stagnates because there seem to be no avenues of additional separation or possible reconciliation left to explore. *Avoiding* additional interaction follows, and finally *terminating* occurs (either through formal divorce or simple attrition). The staircase model is illustrated in Figure 2.2.

Like stairs in a staircase, movement toward intimacy is not random or chaotic; it is systematic and sequential, with early stages laying the foundation for later stages. Knapp and Vangelisti (1991) argued that even couples who may appear to skip stages (e.g., a

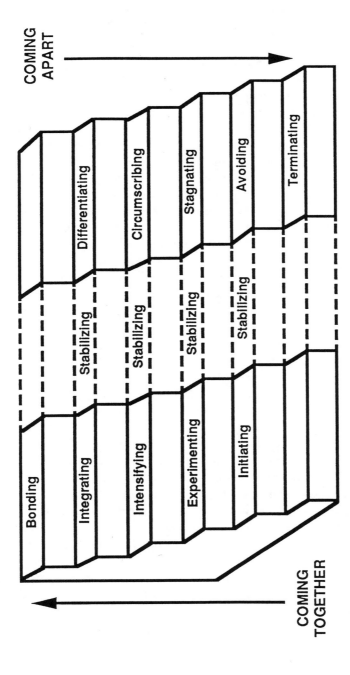

Figure 2.2. A Staircase Model of Relationship Stages

SOURCE: From Interpersonal Communication and Human Relationships (2nd ed., p. 53) by M. L. Knapp and A. L. Vangelisti, 1991, Boston: Allyn & Bacon. Adapted by permission of the authors and the publisher.

weekend romance ending in marriage) eventually will have to recycle and progress through earlier stages.

Likewise, movement away from intimacy is systematic and sequential, a general reversal of the coming together process. This difference is reflected in the correspondence between stages in coming together and coming apart. For example, during the experimenting phase, potential partners are active information seekers, asking questions and self-disclosing in an effort to assess the kind of relationship they want to develop and to determine the best ways to get there. During the stagnating phase, this orientation reverses: Former partners are information avoiders because they believe they know all that is necessary to know. Similarly a parallel but reversed process occurs when the joint identity established during the integrating stage is dismantled during the differentiating stage.

Of course, relationships do not always advance to bonding once they begin forming, nor do they necessarily deteriorate to complete termination when they begin coming apart. As Knapp and Vangelisti (1991) indicated in the model by using "stabilizing" as a midpoint option between each pair of coming together and coming apart steps, some relationships neither progress nor decline beyond a certain point; they simply continue to exist where they are. The "empty marriage" might, for example, signal a relationship that has stagnated but has not terminated through formal divorce.

The staircase model is not without its limitations. For example, like all linear models, it ignores the cyclical movements in relationships as they swing between periods of change and stability or between times of togetherness and separateness (see Baxter, 1990). In addition, if the reversal hypothesis was true, breadth and depth of topics would decrease during relationship deterioration, and conversations would become less personalized and less synchronized. Research suggests, however, that even during relationship disengagement, partners cannot "unknow" each other and thus still are able to predict what the other will say or do. In fact, research shows that breadth of disclosure may diminish systematically, but depth of disclosure actually increases at certain points during disengagement (Baxter, 1983; Tolhuizen, 1986; Tolstedt & Stokes, 1984). Still, Knapp and Vangelisti's model provides a global view that is useful in organizing our thinking about relationships and how, in a general sense, they develop and change. From this perspective we can focus on change that is associated with aspects of self-disclosure.

&. Transformation Agents

To illustrate how self-disclosure and relationships unfold through mutual transformation, we discuss several factors that research studies have identified as important elements in the change process. We refer to these factors as *transformation agents*. They include the relational definition, time, attributional processes, liking, reciprocity, and goals.

In our subsequent discussions, we use the notion of transformation agent as a way to organize the information on disclosure in relationships. As you will see, at most points in the development and deterioration of relationships, many transformation agents may be represented, or only a few. For example, when a couple is attempting to maintain a relationship and keep it viable, time, attributional processes, and reciprocity may all be salient factors in the disclosure-relationship connection. When a relationship has deteriorated, however, the strategic use of self-disclosure to end it may make all other transformation agents irrelevant. In addition, because we are discussing a mutually transformative process, we want to stress that the relationship is a "culture" that both influences and is influenced by the self-disclosure that occurs within it.

Thus the *relational definition* may influence our disclosure. For example, if we are in a marital relationship, our disclosure may be more like a telegram—short and incomplete. But disclosure also may affect the way partners define their relationship with each other. So, when people disclose in certain ways, the recipient may be expected, or be forced, to define the nature of the relationship differently (e.g., nonintimate to intimate).

Time is an interesting transformative agent because, on the one hand, it may seem to be a more objective assessment than relational definition or attributional processes. After all, we have heard parents or television characters remark apathetically, "After 35 years of marriage, what's left to say?" On the other hand, time is a dimension on which events are arrayed. When many events cluster in a short period of time, the "rate of change" for a phenomenon is great. Those same events spread over a longer period of time indicate a slow rate of change. The same is true for how quickly and/or smoothly self-disclosure and relational change occur. Thus two couples may reach the same level of intimacy and commitment after 3 months, but one couple feels as though they have experienced a whirlwind romance, while the other feels as though they have moved gradually and cautiously.

The transformative function also may be seen with *attributional processes*. The choice of disclosing messages may be dependent on attributions that a person makes about his or her relational partner. In addition, the context within which the attributions are made (e.g., context of trust) may influence how much that person is willing to disclose. There is a mutuality between *liking* and disclosure, as there is between *reciprocity* and disclosure in relationships. Finally, when relational partners or friends are strategic, they use disclosure (or avoid disclosing) to achieve personal or relational *goals*.

We also recognize that the transformation agents are not mutually exclusive in nature. Every case has a potential for overlap, but there is enough distinction to reinforce the utility of these categories as a way to understand the mutual transformation process between relationships and disclosure.

Relational Definition

Sarah and Joel had been friends for several months. They were both in their early 20s and had met right after college in their division at work. They liked having lunch together and occasionally even seeing a movie on the weekend. Joel had known for some time that he wanted more out of the relationship than friendship but was afraid to say anything to Sarah. He knew she liked him but didn't know whether she felt any romantic interest in him. One day at lunch she was talking about a man she met over the weekend who asked her out to dinner later in the week. Joel found himself saying something about how she should not date men she doesn't know, how she should think about establishing a friendship first. Sarah took in the advice and then confronted Joel: "Are you telling me these things because you care about me as a friend or because you are jealous that I may find a romantic partner?" Joel felt that the time was right and revealed exactly how he felt about Sarah and what he wanted from the relationship.

The definition of a relationship represents the way partners individually and together think about the relationship and the behaviors that would be appropriate, given that definition. At one level a relationship definition might be as simple as selecting an appropriate "sociological category" into which the relationship falls. These categories might include friends (or best friends), lovers, dating partners, spouses, co-workers, neighbors, and so on.

At another level, however, relationships can be defined by their "salient qualities." These qualities might include any characteristic or combination of characteristics that a couple feels are important in their view of the relationship at a particular time. For example, one couple may believe that their relationship is intimate because they have spent long hours sharing feelings, plans, fears, and so forth; a second couple may believe that their relationship is intimate because they care deeply for each other; and yet a third couple may believe that their relationship is intimate because they have engaged in sexual intercourse. In all but the most superficial and role-guided relationship (e.g., a customer and sales clerk), these definitions emerge and reformulate as partners digest their relationship and attempt to establish guidelines for their own and their partner's behavior.

Patterns of self-disclosure seem to vary across relationships that display differences in definition. For example, Tardy, Hosman, and Bradac (1981) examined differences in college students' disclosure to friends and family. They found that when the target was a same-sex friend, the disclosure was more negative, intimate, honest, and frequent than when the target was a parent. Tardy et al. (1981) noted that perhaps friends and family members are providing different functions regarding disclosures. Clearly the nature of the relational definition is influencing the choices for disclosing messages.

A study by Rosenfeld and Welsh (1985) examined disclosure differences for dual-career and single-career marital couples. They found that, for dual-career couples, the patterns of disclosure are more equal than those for single-career couples. Wives of single-career husbands reported that they disclosed more than their husbands in regard to breadth, depth, and amount of disclosure. Dual-career spouses did not differ on anything except depth. Rosenfeld and Welsh suggested that this finding is consistent with a couple's orientation on more basic issues such as division of household chores and distribution of resources in the relationship. Thus a relational definition that includes role equality (we both have careers and will share both chores and resources) will be manifested in patterns of self-disclosure that violate traditional sex role expectations based on female expressivity and male inexpressivity (see Chapter 3).

Not only does the definition of the relationship influence patterns of self-disclosure but the patterns of disclosure also influence the definition of the relationship. Sometimes the relationship is transformed almost immediately and drastically. This change is most likely when the disclosure is oriented specifically toward the relationship. For example, expressing certain types of emotional states ("I love you" or "I don't love you") and expressing relational intent ("Will you marry me?" or "I want a divorce!") are immediate and explicit bids to transform the relational definition. On other occasions even messages not directly oriented toward the relationship may function to redefine it. For example, if Gabriela and Donato have been friends for years and Gabriela recently reveals that she does not like it when Donato talks about his girlfriends, he will have to consider whether Gabriela's feelings are jealousy and, if so, whether they are to be expected in a "friendship" as he defines it.

Another example is seen in a study conducted by Braithwaite (1991) on disclosure between able-bodied individuals and persons with disabilities. Using face-to-face interviews, she focused on people who had visible physical disabilities (e.g., people in wheelchairs). She answered many questions from her investigation, but the information pertinent to this discussion involves the responses of disabled persons to inappropriate questions from able-bodied individuals. When receiving inappropriate questions about their disability, disabled persons often relied on responses suggesting to the individual that he or she incorrectly defined the nature of their relationship (e.g., "It's none of your business") or communicated responses suggesting that the able-bodied person was defining the relationship according to an erroneous definition.

Disclosure also may be one means by which relationship qualities such as intimacy are manifested and reinforced. According to Waring (1987), "self-disclosure is *one* aspect of how close a couple feels toward one another and thus a factor that could increase the couple's intimacy" (p. 291).

Support for Waring's position can be found in several empirical studies. Waring, Tillman, Frelick, Russell, and Weisz (1980) interviewed a random sample of adults in the general population (16 males, 34 females) about their views on intimacy. These interviews revealed that most people identified "sharing private thoughts, dreams, attitudes, beliefs, and fantasy" (p. 473) as important for intimacy. The authors refer to these elements of self-disclosure as "expressiveness." Other findings related to intimacy were that (a) sexuality is part of intimacy (not a primary part); (b) anger, argument, and criticism are not part of intimacy; (c) identity (self-knowledge and self-esteem) is important for intimacy; and (d) childhood exposure to intimacy, usually through parents, is important. These findings were formalized into an instrument, called the Waring Intimacy Questionnaire, to measure intimacy. Selected items from this scale are provided for examination in Table 2.1.

In a later study of married couples, Chelune, Waring, Vosk, Sultan, and Ogden (1984) found that disclosure was a significant means through which marital couples expressed intimacy (although the study did not answer whether disclosure was an antecedent or a consequent condition for marital intimacy). In addition, the results suggested that the content of the disclosure was important. Positive disclosure statements about the self were positively associated with intimacy, while negative statements were inversely related (as the negative statements increased, the couple's ratings of intimacy decreased).

These studies and others revealing strong associations between intimacy and relational adjustment (e.g., Waring, McElrath, Mitchell, & Derry, 1981) suggest that disclosure is more likely to emerge in certain types of relational environments and subsequently to enhance those relational environments. Unfortunately, in other types of environments, the beneficial cycle of self-disclosure and relationship growth is not actualized. As Jacobson, Waldron, and Moore (1980) discovered, couples actually select different behaviors to notice, depending on their level of happiness in the relationship. In a study comparing nondistressed and distressed couples, Jacobson et al. found that nondistressed couples based their daily ratings of satisfaction on positive spouse behaviors (e.g., "Spouse talked about

Table 2.1 Measuring Intimacy

Instructions: The items below represent the types of statements that are found in the Waring Intimacy Questionnaire. The Waring Intimacy Questionnaire is designed to assess marriage, so we have adapted the items to read more generally about relationships. Thus the word *marriage* has been replaced here with the word *relationship*, and the word *spouse* has been replaced with the word *partner*. Therefore, if you are dating, engaged, or married, you will be able to complete the sample questionnaire. We have selected three items to represent each of the eight dimensions that underlie the full 90-item original questionnaire.

Decide how true each of these statements is in your current relationship. Using the 5-point scale provided below, place an appropriate number in the blank by each item.

> 1 = not at all true; never happens
> 2 = slightly true; happens once in a while
> 3 = somewhat true; happens about half the time
> 4 = mostly true; happens quite often
> 5 = completely true; happens all the time

_____ 1. Differences in opinion never lead to verbal abuse in our relationship.
_____ 2. I am at my best when we are together.
_____ 3. Without my relationship my life would lack meaning.
_____ 4. I often feel insecure in social situations.
_____ 5. I wish my partner enjoyed more the activities I enjoy.
_____ 6. If there is one thing that my partner and I are good at, it's talking about our feelings to each other.
_____ 7. It is a real effort for me to try to get along with my partner's parents.
_____ 8. Sometimes sex seems more like work than play to me.
_____ 9. Often I only pretend to listen when my partner talks.
_____10. Discussing problems with my partner seldom leads to arguments.
_____11. I feel that there is distance between my partner and me.
_____12. I have a strong sense of who I am.
_____13. Despite being in a relationship, I often feel lonely.
_____14. Sex with my partner has never been as exciting as in my fantasies.
_____15. We are lucky to have relatives to whom we can go for help.
_____16. I don't really care whether my partner supports me or not, just as long as he/she lets me lead my own life.
_____17. I never hit below the belt when we argue.
_____18. I enjoy spending time with my partner's family.
_____19. My partner rarely turns away from my sexual advances.
_____20. I would be willing to compromise my beliefs to make our relationship better.
_____21. When I compare myself to most other people, I like myself.
_____22. My partner and I share the same goals in life.
_____23. My partner and I like to do things for self-improvement together.
_____24. I can say anything I want to my partner.

Scoring

To score your responses, follow the steps listed below.

1. *Reverse Scores:* Because some items are stated negatively, you will need to reverse the scores you gave to them. These items are number 4, 5, 7, 8, 9, 11, 13, 14, and 20. When you reverse the scores, a score of 1 becomes a 5, a score of 2 becomes a 4, and so on (a score of 3 does not change).

2. *Compute Subscales:*

Add scores for items 1, 10, 17	Total Confl. Resol.	=	____
Add scores for items 5, 22, 23	Total Compatibility	=	____
Add scores for items 4, 12, 21	Total Identity	=	____
Add scores for items 6, 9, 24	Total Expressiveness	=	____
Add scores for items 7, 15, 18	Total Autonomy	=	____
Add scores for items 3, 16, 20	Total Cohesion	=	____
Add scores for items 8, 14, 19	Total Sexuality	=	____
Add scores for items 2, 11, 13	Total Affection	=	____

3. *Compute Total Intimacy:*

Add all of the values for the subscale scores.

Total Intimacy   =   ____

4. *What is your relationship profile?*

Consider these definitions of the subscales provided by Waring and his colleagues:

Conflict Resolution:	The ease with which differences of opinion are resolved
Compatibility:	The degree to which the couple is able to work and play together comfortably
Identity:	Level of self-confidence and self-esteem
Expressiveness:	The degree to which thoughts, beliefs, attitudes, and feelings are shared within the relationship as well as the general level of self-disclosure
Autonomy:	The success with which the couple gains independence from their families of origin and their offspring
Cohesion:	Feeling of commitment to the relationship
Sexuality:	The degree to which sexual needs are communicated and fulfilled by the relationship
Affection:	The degree to which feelings of emotional closeness are expressed by the couple

For any of the subscales, your score could range from a low of 3 to a high of 15. How does your relationship stack up? Look at the definitions for each of the subscales. Are you surprised by the ones that you rated high? Are you surprised by the ones that you rated low? Are there any aspects of intimacy that you think this questionnaire does not measure? You might ask your partner to complete the scale, and then compare your scores.

SOURCE: Adapted from the Waring Intimacy Questionnaire (Form 90) by E. M. Waring, Department of Psychiatry, Queen's University, Kingston, Ontario, Canada. Copyright 1979 by E. M. Waring. Used by permission.

personal feelings" and "Spouse showed interest in what I said by agreeing or asking relevant questions"). By contrast, distressed couples oriented their satisfaction ratings toward negative spouse behaviors (e.g., "Spouse interrupted me" and "Spouse dominated the conversation").

In sum, the theme found throughout the literature on intimacy and disclosure points to considering their association to be a process of mutual influence (Chelune, Robinson, & Kommor, 1984; Reis & Shaver, 1988; Waring & Chelune, 1983). This conclusion is consistent with the perspective guiding this section: Self-disclosure and relationship definitions are mutually transformative.

The next transformation agent to be discussed is *time*. As you will see, time and relational definition are not necessarily mutually exclusive, because definitions tend to unfold over time. Still, enough differentiation can be made to be useful in understanding the transformative aspects of time.

Time

> When Andy and Gladys first met, they spent many hours sharing their past, their views of the future, their feelings, hopes, joys, failures, and what they wanted to experience in their marriage. After 25 years of marriage, much less time is spent disclosing. What they share now, to the amusement of their teenage children, are stories from their shared past that they retell together—correcting each other, embellishing, co-creating each event. "She was so mad at me she could have spit," says Andy. "Yes," says Gladys, "and if you hadn't taken the car keys, I would have driven out of your life forever." "Oh, you couldn't live without me," laughs Andy, and they both smile. They seem to recognize that traumatic events take on a different perspective if allowed to become an accepted part of the fabric of the relationship history.

Relationships develop over time. People meet, talk, separate, talk to others, think about their interactions, meet again, talk again, and so on. Interestingly, there are some features of relationships that only time can put in perspective. This is a difficult concept, but think about time as a string and the interactions of a couple as different types of beads on that string. Over time, a pattern will emerge in which some beads begin repeating on the string and others appear only rarely. As a couple looks at its own "string of beads," they will find either comfort or boredom in the repetition. They will find the rare beads to be frightening or exciting. They will expect certain patterns at the beginning of the relationship, but not later. A couple might even orient to the string of beads according to whether their movement is toward coming together or coming apart (Knapp & Vangelisti, 1991).

Thus the meaning and function of disclosure is transformed by the time frame over which the disclosure has been given. Like beads on a string, repeated themes in one's disclosure can be either comforting or boring to one's partner. For example, a young woman might tell her friend about a new boyfriend, with the enthusiastic endorsement, "He's so open; he tells me everything he feels." Two months later, if she has become tired of playing the active listener role, she might say, "He is no fun; all he does is talk about himself and his problems." The young man's messages may not have changed, but playing the role of receiver for his disclosure has become tedious for the young woman over time. Even the meaning of self-disclosure can change over time. A statement such as "I don't feel like my life is going anywhere" will be heard with sympathy and support in an emerging romantic relationship between two college students who are anxious to leave school and begin their careers. Thirty years later, the same statement could be taken as a strong indictment of the marriage and its future. In a sense the statement no longer functions as a statement about the self, but as a statement about the relationship.

Social penetration theory, developed by Irwin Altman and Dalmas Taylor (1973), presents an analysis of how time influences disclosure and the life cycle of a relationship. Since its introduction into the interpersonal attraction literature in the early 1970s, social penetration theory has been one of the most widely accepted descriptions of how disclosure functions in the development of relationships. It forms the basis of several models of relationship development, most notably Knapp and Vangelisti's (1991) staircase model (described earlier) and Levinger's (1983) model of relationship formation.

Social penetration theory is based on the assumption that relationships intensify gradually and in an orderly fashion, paralleling the development in message exchange from superficial to intimate topics and from a narrow to a broad range of topics. It implies that people come into relationships as intact, fully formed entities whose inner cores are revealed through successively deeper revelations, much as an onion is unpeeled by layers. Being willing to reciprocate self-disclosure allows people to test successively deeper levels of disclosure and thereby to build trust in incremental steps over time (Altman & Taylor, 1973). In principle at least, there is no necessary end point for this progression of increasing breadth and depth.

This early version of social penetration theory is closely tied to the common notion of time moving forward. It predicted that people "reveal" themselves gradually over time and that relationships develop in a parallel fashion along the trajectory of increasing intimacy. As we have indicated throughout this chapter, however, people are not fully formed entities with a static body of information that they selectively reveal to a partner until they are "known" to the other person. Rather, people change constantly, and the information that an individual considers to be self-disclosure will depend on the attitudes of his or her partner and their mutually created relational environment (see Baxter, 1991). Furthermore, increasing evidence from longitudinal research (research that follows the same couples over time) suggests that the linear progression assumed by social penetration is only one possible pattern for self-disclosure over time. There are at least three other patterns.

The first alternative pattern might be described as a typical linear progression at first but shifting to a sharp decline. It appears that, for some couples, a sharp decline in disclosure occurs after the initial period of openness. In a rather dramatic depiction of variation in the supposed progressive movement of relationships toward greater openness, Huston, McHale, and Crouter (1986) found that after only 1 year of marriage, couples showed less affection and were less approving and disclosing than they had been as newlyweds. They also spent less time talking about their relationship, said "I love you" less often, and disclosed their wants and concerns less often. These findings are interesting because the couples had relatively satisfying relationships overall. It seems that self-disclosure, like other types of activities, sometimes recedes into the background, giving way to newer, more pressing concerns for developing relationships. This pattern can be seen in the first graph in Figure 2.3.

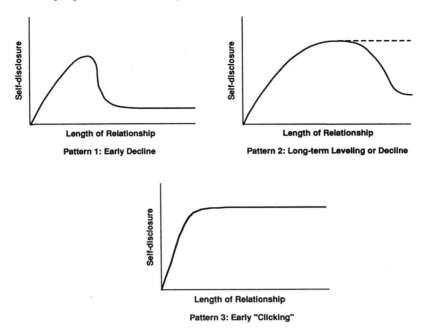

Figure 2.3. Three Alternative Patterns of Self-Disclosure Over Time

A second alternative pattern might be described as a trajectory of increasing disclosure that eventually levels off and sometimes even declines. Research on long-term marriages shows a leveling off in the importance of disclosure for marital stability. Hendrick (1981) found that disclosure was a good predictor of marital satisfaction both for individuals and for couples but was negatively related to years of marriage. Hendrick speculated that disclosure becomes less important to a couple when they have been married for a long time, know each other well, and are satisfied in their relationship. Gilbert (1977) speculated a bit less optimistically that long-term relationships are psychologically and emotionally enmeshed and that partners are vulnerable to significant pain from certain types of disclosure. These circumstances, she argued, often contribute to a curvilinear pattern for disclosure over time (a slower rate and then decrease). This pattern is seen in the second graph in Figure 2.3.

A third alternative pattern might be described as a kind of "clicking" trajectory, where disclosure normally seen in long-term relationships develops almost immediately rather than gradually over time. Berg and his colleagues, over a series of studies using friends, roommates, and dating partners, found evidence that relationships sometimes just "click" from the very start rather than becoming close over time. Longitudinal analyses revealed that couples who stayed together had these early disclosure patterns (even within the first few weeks). These patterns were not found in the relationships that did not continue (Berg, 1984; Berg & Clark, 1986; Berg & McQuinn, 1986; Hays, 1985). This rapid rise in self-disclosure very early in the relationship is reflected in the third graph in Figure 2.3.

To explain these findings, Berg invoked the notion of "schemata" —mental structures that help people within cultures organize the behavior they observe and produce, to give it meaning. Relational schemata contain understandings of what should be expected to happen in certain types of relationships—for example, types of goals we might reasonably be expected to set, behaviors we are expected to display to meet those goals, signals of our intentions to other people, and interpretations of the behaviors of others (Baxter, 1987; Berg & Clark, 1986).

According to Berg and Clark (1986), people make very rapid assessments of the extent to which a new relationship fits their "prototype" of a close relationship. A particular schema or script may be applied because some aspect of a current situation or interaction resembles central aspects of that schema or script. A person then begins acting as though all of the attributes of a schema were, in fact, present. Thus even very early interactions may be synchronous and highly disclosing. In effect, some couples do not need to interact over time to build a relationship; rather, they recognize key elements of a relationship in their interactions and then fill in the rest before it ever occurs. The beads on their string of time are few, but they are very important.

In sum, relational events occur over time; some are affected by self-disclosure, and some are not. Findings inconsistent with traditional social penetration theory suggest that self-disclosure and close relationships do not necessarily develop over time in a parallel, incremental, and continuous fashion. People may wish to believe so and therefore may report a sequential progression on questionnaire surveys when they reconstruct their relationship from memory. However, research done with couples over time indicates that temporal patterns are, in fact, flexible and varied.

Attributional Processes

> Craig, Bill, and Todd, high school juniors, were sitting at a table in the lunchroom after school, waiting for basketball practice to be over so that they could get a ride home with a friend. Eventually another junior, Rick, joined the group. When the conversation turned to families, Rick expressed his frustration with his stepfather and the breakup, in Rick's eyes, of a previously happy family unit with just his sister, mother, and himself. After Rick left, Craig remarked that Rick was a little weird for talking so intimately about family problems. However, Bill said that he thought Rick just saw them as friendly and trustworthy. Todd concurred and added that he felt good that Rick was comfortable talking about something personal with them.

People are not passive receivers of information from or about their partners (Duck, 1982). They make attributions that influence and are influenced by their shared relational environment (Bradbury & Fincham, 1989; Derlega, Winstead, Wong, & Greenspan, 1987). When the relationship is casual or new and the relational environment is uncluttered, people tend to make one of two kinds of attributions about another person's disclosure: *dispositional attributions* (e.g., Fred told me about his drinking problem because he is a generally open person who never keeps things back) and *situational attributions* (e.g., Audrey told me about her grades because she just found out she may not graduate and is extremely upset right now). When the relational environment is multilayered and complex because of shared experiences and intertwined goals, couples also make *interpersonal attributions* (Newman, 1981) (e.g., John told me about his mother's behavior so that after we get married I won't act the same way toward him; I can't seem to make Cindy happy; Bill won't let me do it).

The attributions we use to explain why someone is telling us something intimate or revealing are an important part of what the self-disclosure will mean to the relationship. When our attributions lead us to believe that the discloser considers us to be special and that only we are receiving this disclosure, we tend to increase our feelings of attraction for that individual (Taylor, Gould, & Brounstein, 1981) and to feel that we have a special relationship with him or her (Baile, 1984). Reciprocally, when we want to sustain or intensify a relationship, we are likely to make positive attributions about the disclosure (Derlega, Winstead, Wong, & Greenspan, 1987).

This feeling of being special generalizes even to relationships long established. Shimanoff (1987) examined disclosure of negative emotions in marriage. She created scenarios that depicted disclosure of one of two types of emotion: vulnerability ("You hurt my feelings when you do that") or hostility ("I'm mad at you"). The object of these emotions was either one's spouse or some other person, such as a co-worker or a friend. She found that when spouses received disclosures of vulnerability and hostility about another person, they reported enhanced feelings of intimacy toward their partner. When they received these disclosures about themselves, they reported lower intimacy. Shimanoff suggested that receiving negative information about others may create a "we versus they" orientation in the relationship and increase attributions of closeness. By contrast, those same messages, when directed toward one's spouse, are face threatening and make a couple feel (at least temporarily) separate.

As indicated by Shimanoff's (1987) research, when marital couples communicate negative emotional disclosures about their partners, these messages result in negative attributions and feelings. Often the emotional disclosures may be communicated in the form of a complaint. In Shimanoff's (1987) scheme, these complaint messages may be seen as vulnerabilities or as hostilities directed toward the partner.

Alberts (1988) explored complaint messages directed toward one's partner and the types of responses partners gave to these messages. Her analysis compared adjusted and maladjusted couples (as indicated by scores on the Spanier Dyadic Adjustment Scale; Spanier, 1976) who had been married or living together for at least 6 months. She found that the adjusted and maladjusted couples differed on several issues. The adjusted couples tended to offer more behavioral complaints—statements such as "Why haven't we had a cooked meal all week?"—compared to the maladjusted couples, who offered more personal characteristics complaints, such as, "You're a snob." The adjusted couples used more positive affect when delivering these complaints. For the adjusted couples, the receiving partner responded with more agreement responses, such as, "Yes, you are right about that," than the maladjusted couples; the maladjusted couples, by contrast, responded with more countercomplaints.

Further, Alberts (1988) found that the critical variable influencing the type of response a partner gave after receiving a complaint was the type of relationship the couple was in (adjusted/maladjusted). In fact, the type of relationship was more important than either the complaint type or the complaint affect. As Alberts (1988) noted, "It could be that in such intimate relationships as romance and marriage one's feelings about one's partner color one's communication behavior more strongly than that partner's immediate [complaint] behavior" (p. 193).

In thinking about the issue of constructing complaints or indicating to our partners that we are dissatisfied or unhappy about their behavior, we may prepare ourselves for disclosure and subsequent attributions from our partners by using "imagined interactions" (Rosenblatt & Meyer, 1986). When individuals reveal personal information through disclosure, they may feel vulnerable to the responses of the other. Clearly there is some risk in telling personal feelings, regardless of how well we might know someone (Rawlins, 1983). By using imagined interactions, we might practice the presentation of the information, anticipating the outcome. By doing so, we can shape our messages in ways that might minimize the vulnerability we feel.

Rosenblatt and Meyer (1986) proposed this concept and discussed the utility of imagined interactions. They noted that through imagined interactions we can figure out ways to solve problems or enter into pretend dialogues with others that could not actually take place. By doing so, we can either prepare for upcoming interactions in which we need to disclose risky information or play out exchanges that might cause too much vulnerability for us if we actually had the conversation.

Rosenblatt and Meyer (1986) pointed out that using this technique of imagined interactions may help clarify our own feelings, while also getting ourselves ready for actual exchanges of disclosure. By using imagined interactions, we may influence the subsequent attributional process that others engage in on hearing our disclosures.

As this section has shown, there are many issues regarding the attributional process and its connection to disclosure within relationships. At the most general level, we can say that attributing self-disclosure to something special about us, about the discloser, or about the relationship we have with the discloser makes the experience a positive one. We feel attracted to the person disclosing and are likely to reciprocate the disclosure. A number of variables, however, can influence what might seem to be a simple model of how the reasons we attribute for someone's disclosure input affect how much we like him or her and, in turn, how much we self-disclose. For instance, some chronically lonely people tend to make negative self-attributions ("I'm not good with people") and thereby view the disclosure they receive as somehow accidental or mistaken (Young, 1982). In addition, some people with a great many friends, regardless of the attributions they make, do not respond encouragingly to self-disclosure because they choose not to expand their social network.

Liking

> Margaret, a 30-year-old nurse, had worked at the same hospital for several years. She enjoyed the daily interaction with her co-workers and tried to be a supportive colleague. Jill was a much younger nurse who had joined the staff recently. One day while Margaret and Jill were sharing a cup of coffee during break, Jill began to talk about her marriage and her husband's abusive patterns toward her and her children. At first Margaret tried to listen politely but eventually stopped Jill from going on and excused herself. Later Margaret told her husband, "I felt so uncomfortable. I hardly know her, and she's telling me all this stuff. I think she needs help. Finally I told her to go to the hospital social services office and talk to someone there."

It may seem to be common sense that disclosure leads to liking because most people are more comfortable around people they know (uncertainty is low) than people they do not know (uncertainty is high) (Berger, 1987). Although this notion is generally true, there are qualifications to the disclosure-liking relationship (see Collins & Miller, 1991, for a review).

First, disclosing behavior that violates normative expectations will not lead to liking. People are more comfortable when interactions —especially initial interactions—are smooth and normative. Any actions that violate the routinized unfolding of early interactions will make people appear less attractive. In a review of the self-disclosure literature, Bochner (1982) and Parks (1982) both concluded that moderately intimate, positive, and well-timed disclosure (late in an interaction and preferably after the initial interaction) could enhance attraction and liking but that highly personal, negative disclosure given too soon inhibits liking unless some strong initial attraction already exists.

Second, liking is a function of how the dyad perceives the disclosure, not simply how much or how widely a particular person discloses. Miller (1990) examined whether sorority women who typically disclose are generally liked. She found that premise not to be true; she found no effect due to an individual's overall tendency to disclose (no individual effect). She did, however, find a relationship effect; that is, individuals who disclosed highly intimate information across the board to others, as compared to those who disclosed very little, were not more likely to be liked. Instead highly intimate disclosure was positively associated only with liking for partners who had a special relationship with one another (e.g., they were close friends).

Third, people may overestimate how much they disclose to people they like because members of our society *believe it is appropriate* to engage in high levels of self-disclosure with people they like (Bochner, 1982; Shapiro & Swenson, 1969). Consequently, when asked to indicate whether they would disclose to a person they like (e.g., a good friend) versus a person they do not like, most people report greater disclosure to the well-liked target. This finding does not mean, however, that people actually disclose more, only that they report they "probably would" or "probably do" disclose more. Observations of actual behavior indicate that people may be guarded about expressing their feelings, even—or especially—to close others. Levinger and Senn (1967), for example, found that, in satisfied couples, negative feelings about important matters typically were not expressed. In fact, during their conversations, satisfied couples often display a tacit norm of nondisclosure by not asking directly about their partners' feelings but by probing indirectly and "mind reading" (Gottman, 1979).

It seems that satisfied couples agree (probably unconsciously) to allow each other the privacy of their thoughts and engage in conversations on the assumption that everything is fine. Asking questions might unnecessarily raise issues that would be problematic. Consistent with this view, Levinger and Breedlove (1966) found that perceived agreement was a more important factor in marital satisfaction than was actual agreement.

Fourth, disclosure will not lead to liking if it is responded to in a negative manner. Because most disclosure emerges during ongoing interaction, speakers look for cues that it was received in the spirit intended and that it has been regarded as appropriate. When self-disclosure is ignored, diminished, or otherwise dismissed, the discloser feels disconfirmed or even rejected (Bavelas, 1983). When self-disclosure is received positively and is responded to with sensitivity and understanding, it generally leads to attraction (Miller & Berg, 1984).

The set of cues that signal receptivity to and appreciation for another's self-disclosure is known as *conversational responsiveness* (Berg, 1987; Miller & Berg, 1984). According to Miller and Berg's (1984) original formulation, conversational responsiveness refers to "behaviors made by the recipient of another's communication through which the recipient indicates interest in and understanding of that communication" (p. 193). Listeners display responsiveness to another's self-disclosure in the content, style, and timing of their responses. The *content* of a response refers to *what* is said—for example, elaborations on the same topic or comparable disclosure. The *style* of a response refers to *how* something is said—for example, with intensity and enthusiasm rather than apathy and reluctance. Style typically is recognized in the nonverbal behaviors of communicators, such as eye gaze, body lean, and head nods. The *timing* of a response refers to how soon after the self-disclosure is received that the response is given. In general, long silences and conversational lapses before responding would indicate lower responsiveness.

Summarizing the mutually transformative functions of self-disclosure and liking is difficult. Under some conditions self-disclosing will lead to liking; under other conditions, however, it leads to not liking. This assertion is especially true when the disclosure is given too early and is too negative. But even early disclosure and negative disclosure will be received positively if some degree of liking already exists. Perhaps the safest claim to make is that several transformation agents intervene in the relationship between self-disclosure and liking.

Reciprocity

> Winona did not participate very much in college activities. She wasn't married, but she was 24 years old and worked as a waitress 25 hours per week to pay for her tuition and other expenses. She always felt a little different from the other students in her classes. Then one day she was assigned to do group work with four or five of her classmates. After class, she and a woman named Melanie happened to walk out together. During the conversation in the hall, Melanie revealed that she was a single parent raising her 3-year old-daughter all alone. Winona found herself describing her own situation in response to Melanie's opening. As they parted, Melanie and Winona both felt a keen sense of equal sharing and mutual respect.

To reciprocate means to give something back that matches something received. It is common in most cultures to reciprocate a resource, a commodity, a gesture of goodwill, or some form of assistance that has been received. Early research in self-disclosure with paired strangers in controlled laboratory studies produced evidence of a similar phenomenon: the dyadic effect, or norm of reciprocity. In self-disclosure research, the *norm of reciprocity* refers to the tendency for recipients to match the level of intimacy in the disclosure they return with the level of intimacy in the disclosure they receive. For example, if Scott reveals to Jane that he has a problem with alcohol and Jane chooses to reciprocate, she would refer to her own problems with alcohol or other substances. To refer to her love of chocolate as a similar addiction would trivialize Scott's disclosure (unless perhaps Jane is clinically overweight or diabetic).

The traditional explanation for the norm of reciprocity is to say that it results from the desire of individuals to maintain equity of exchange (to equalize both the rewards and the risks of self-disclosure).

However, alternative views attribute reciprocity to the more global constraints of conversational norms.

Although we are not often consciously aware of conversational norms, they help us know when it is our turn to speak, and they help us know the kinds of comments that would be appropriate, given the topic on the floor. The requirement to be topically relevant is quite binding, and violations are noticed by other speakers (Grice, 1975). For example, if you have ever said to someone, "So what's your point?" during a conversation, chances are he or she failed to make it clear how his or her comment connected to the topic being discussed. When a speaker self-discloses, the recipient has to generate a response that is not only sensitive to the discloser's self-imposed vulnerability but also responsive to the conversational demand to be topically relevant. The recipient may find that self-disclosing in return addresses both needs.

Interestingly some evidence suggests that maintaining topical relevance is even more important when the disclosure is highly intimate than when it is not. Berg and Archer (1983) established several possible stimulus conditions and response sets to see how speakers who responded in certain ways to disclosing messages would be rated on social attractiveness. The authors found that for *low intimacy input* conditions, speakers who reciprocated both intimacy and topic were rated as socially attractive. For *high intimacy input* conditions, however, speakers who reciprocated the topic but not the intimacy were rated as socially unattractive.

Regardless of the motivation underlying the phenomenon, it appears that several variables influence the likelihood that a recipient will return an equivalent disclosure. One important variable is the recipient's perception of why he or she was chosen to receive the disclosure. As mentioned previously, recipients make attributions about the source of the disclosure and the source's motivations. These attributions then mediate between the disclosure received and offered in return (Derlega, Winstead, Wong, & Greenspan, 1987). Reciprocity is more likely when the recipient makes positive attributions and judges the disclosure received to be rewarding. For example, reciprocity is probable when the recipient feels special ("She is telling me this because she trusts me"), when the recipient feels positive toward the character of the discloser ("His intention is to help me understand why he fears commitment so I won't think it's just me"), and/or when the recipient feels that the relationship is special. The influence of attributions has been used to explain why self-disclosure given late in an interaction (compared to early) is responded to more favorably: Late disclosure is interpreted by the recipient as a signal that the revealer waited until the interaction was personalized (He/she got to know me first). Disclosure given too early invites negative attributions because it seems to be indiscriminate. (See Chapter 4 for an extended discussion of timing as it relates to self-disclosure of "negative" information about the self.)

A second variable that influences the likelihood of reciprocity is the relational goal of the recipient. Attributions may be quite positive, but because the recipient does not want to develop a relationship, adhering to a norm of equitable exchange may not be important. To reciprocate the disclosure would possibly lead the other person to perceive a developing level of intimacy that was not actually present. Conversely, if the recipient wants to develop or enhance a relationship, he or she may choose not to reciprocate because the risk to the relationship simply would be too great (e.g., we occasionally will tell a total stranger information we would never risk telling a significant other). In such cases the recipient still may display responsiveness but not offer his or her own disclosure. Finally, if the goal is to de-escalate or terminate a relationship, failure to reciprocate or even to be responsive over repeated occasions will eventually signal to the other person that his or her disclosure is no longer rewarding. More will be said about relational goals in the next section.

A third variable that exerts a profound influence on patterns of reciprocity is the developmental stage of the relationship (Altman, 1973). Among strangers, for whom judgments of competence rest on displays of normative behavior and for whom small tests of trustworthiness need to be assessed quickly, the desire to reciprocate self-disclosure at a comparable level is strong. Among friends and other types of developed relationships, however, disclosure need not be reciprocated except in the broad sense of being willing to exchange the listener role periodically; there is less need to reciprocate intimate self-disclosure immediately and during the same interaction.

Because friends already have developed a level of trust and confidence in each other, they do not need to demonstrate that trust by reciprocating each time. They can "take turns" engaging in intimate disclosure during the course of their friendship. Derlega, Wilson, and Chaikin (1976) demonstrated this phenomenon in a study of female college students. Subjects received a note that was high or low in intimate disclosure from either a friend or a stranger (actually an experimental confederate). Results showed that when subjects received a note from a stranger, they gave back a note that matched the one received in high or low intimacy. However, when subjects received a note from a friend, they gave back a low intimacy note, regardless of the level they received.

The need to reciprocate immediately seems to be low for married couples as well. Rosenfeld and Bowen (1991) found a fairly low correlation (low degree of reciprocity) between husbands' and wives' self-ratings of disclosure. They also found that a spouse's own level of self-disclosure is a stronger predictor of his or her marital satisfaction than the level of self-disclosure of his or her marital partner. Rosenfeld and Bowen offered several explanations for these findings. It may be that people who are very satisfied in their marriage are also likely to engage in high levels of disclosure. It also may be, however, that in long-term relationships the perception that one has the opportunity to engage freely in disclosure with a partner who is willing to act as a good listener is more likely to lead to satisfaction than is the reciprocal exchange of disclosure. Of course, the authors warn that if levels of disclosure are too different for too long, it may "eventually result in relationship stress for both spouses if the actions of the nondisclosing spouse limit the couple's ability to establish a relationship that both spouses define as equitable or just" (Rosenfeld & Bowen, 1991, p. 81).

So far, our discussion has presumed that the recipient of self-disclosure is free to decide whether to reciprocate. However, sometimes this choice is severely curtailed by the person who sends the disclosing messages. Thus a fourth variable intervening in the reciprocation process is whether the discloser will *allow* the other person a chance to reciprocate with personal information.

Vangelisti, Knapp, and Daly (1990) investigated a construct relevant to this point, called "conversational narcissism." The conversational narcissist uses strategies such as boasting, asking questions to demonstrate superior knowledge without showing interest in the receiver's response, engaging in one-upping the other person's disclosures without giving serious consideration to the information disclosed and perhaps interrupting the exchange, shifting the conversational focus to him- or herself, and overusing "I" statements. As the conversational narcissist dominates the interaction of others to remain continually the center of attention, the norm of reciprocity may be hampered significantly.

This discussion of reciprocity indicates critical concerns in understanding the way reciprocity, disclosure, and significant relationships interact. An important summary point is that reciprocity is "normative," meaning it is a common and expected occurrence but is not invariant or automatic. As a general rule, people do feel some obligation to respond appropriately to another person's self-disclosure, but the form and timing of that response will vary. One particularly important element in determining how and when a response is given is the goals of the relationship partners.

Goals

> David and Ingrid were married in 1975. The marriage deteriorated to the point where David wanted to leave the relationship. He began to close up to Ingrid. He no longer talked about his feelings or shared his concerns with her. The interactions between them had stagnated to the point where small talk was about all they did. Despite Ingrid's insistence that he open up to her, David would not. He knew that eventually she would get tired of the struggle and give him the divorce he wanted.

People may be attempting to reach many types of goals when they disclose information to others. They may wish (a) to achieve some degree of catharsis (Stiles, 1987), (b) to present a positive, likable, or true image of themselves (Schlenker, 1984), (c) to gain information from others (Berger & Bradac, 1982), or (d) to signal how they want a relationship to be defined (Baxter, 1979; Miell & Duck, 1986). Rosenfeld and Kendrick (1984) found that, for college students, the most frequently cited goals of self-disclosure with friends were relationship maintenance/enhancement, self-clarification, and reciprocity (opportunities for disclosing back).

An interesting study of how disclosure is used strategically in friendship development was conducted by Miell and Duck (1986). They analyzed responses to several open-ended questions regarding appropriate behaviors for various relationship goals—for example, making a new acquaintance, intensifying a relationship, restricting a relationship's development, and interacting with a close friend. Responses revealed that behaviors toward a new partner ("someone who has just been met but who could become a friend") were motivated by two fundamental aims: (a) to delay revealing too much about oneself, and (b) to gain information about the other person and to assess his or her promise as a partner. Interestingly, some behaviors are identical for both the getting acquainted goals of a new relationship and for the restricting goals of a developed relationship. Figure 2.4 shows, for example, that being reserved and polite may be used as a positive and encouraging behavior in the new partner "script" but may be used as a negative and discouraging behavior in the restricting "script." Other behaviors become reversed between the scripts, however, such that questions are not asked, responses are not given, and partner's reactions are not observed.

Miell and Duck's (1986) findings indicate that disclosing behaviors, disclosure-eliciting behaviors, and disclosure-avoiding behaviors cannot be fully understood apart from their relational context. This theme is evident again in the way disclosure is used for disengaging from a relationship. In fact, other than very explicit revelations, patterns of self-disclosures given, withheld, and not reciprocated must unfold over time. They are highly dependent on the ability of partners to notice and interpret them. Often, in fact, dissatisfied partners do not even realize they are sabotaging their relationship; they may feel themselves withdrawing but do not actually recognize their termination goals until confronted.

The media are replete with examples of the revelation scene during relationship disengagement in which a desperate spouse finally cries, "I don't love you, and I never loved you. Our marriage is a pathetic sham, and I want out." This is a very direct use of self-disclosure as a *disengagement strategy.*

Probably a more common scenario is one in which patterns of self-disclosure change gradually over time and take their meaning from subtle changes in the couple's understanding of their relationship's health and stability. For example, actions that normally might be seen as polite regard for one's privacy get reinterpreted as coldness and distance during times of relational stress. Questions normally seen as expressions of interest are seen as invasive. Topics that a couple typically personalized during conversation get trivialized, or topics that were trivial become personalized.

Baxter (1987) systematized the strategic use of self-disclosure during disengagement by examining how it functions during three stages: private decision making, decision implementation, and public presentation.

In the *private decision-making stage* partners are trying to decide whether to stay in the relationship. They alter their self-disclosure in order to assess factors that might influence their decision. For example, they might use an "endurance test" in which they subject their partner to depersonalized, strangerlike talk to see whether their partner reacts with expressions of affection or intensified commitment. Or a potential disengager might use an "indirect suggestion test," in which he or she hints at a possible disengagement in order to test the waters. These indirect techniques will be used, according to Baxter, until they are no longer functional for gaining additional information. They will not be used if the potential disengager does not have the skills to implement them or does not have sufficient investment in the goal of saving face to exert the effort.

In the *decision implementation stage*, partners attempt to make public their decision to exit the relationship. This knowledge initiates the actual disengagement process, which leads generally to termination unless repair is achieved. According to Baxter, two general strategies are used: distance cuing (significantly reducing the valence, breadth, and depth of personal self-disclosure) and relationship talk cuing (explicit discussion of the state of the relationship and how one feels). A potential disengager will select the more indirect distance cuing if the relationship is not very close. Distance cuing is not very efficient and could cause protracted and ultimately more painful separation. In close relationships, there is an expectation

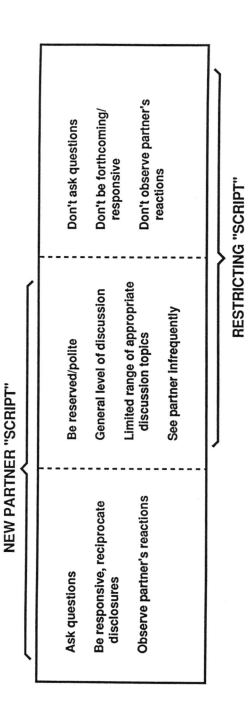

Figure 2.4. Four "Scripts" for Appropriate Behavior

SOURCE: From "Strategies in Developing Friendships" by D. Miell and S. Duck, (p. 134), in V. J. Derlega and B. A. Winstead (Eds.), *Friendship and Social Interaction*, 1986, New York: Springer-Verlag. Reprinted by permission of the authors and the publisher.

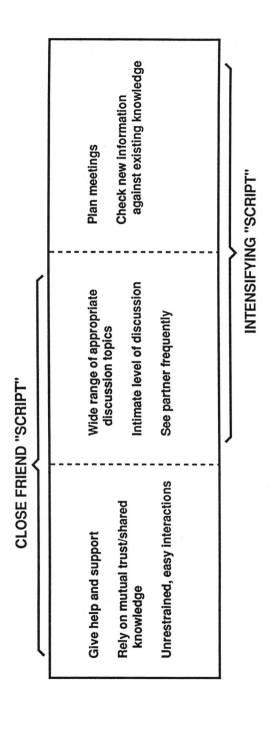

Figure 2.4. Continued

41

that one is owed a more direct accounting for the dissolution. In addition, the accounting will be more direct if the cause of breakup is external to the relationship rather than attributable to the personality or behavior of the partner.

During the *public presentation stage*, disclosure is used to provide accounts to social networks about why the termination was desired (Duck, 1982; La Gaipa, 1982). As Harvey, Weber, and Orbuch (1990) observed, these accounts are a special type of self-disclosure. They are an attempt to impose order on what might seem like a chaotic set of circumstances. They will be a mixture of descriptive and evaluative disclosure, in ratios appropriate to the audiences for whom they are performed.

Conclusions

Self-disclosure plays a critical role in the formation, maintenance, and disengagement of relationships. In this chapter we have attempted to organize a vast body of information according to six transformation agents: relational definition, time, attributional processes, liking, reciprocity, and strategic goals.

Each of these agents, alone and in combination with other agents, provides couples with "guidelines" that tell them when to disclose, why to disclose, and what disclosure means in certain contexts. These guidelines are in constant revision as the agents change. Thus a *relational definition* that changes from casual friends to close friends will expand the range and depth of allowable topics but relax the expectation of immediate *reciprocity*. Ironically a *goal* of disengaging from a relationship also might be achieved by delaying reciprocity—but over such a long period that it signals disregard for relational equivalence. In this second case, *time* becomes the salient indicator.

Obviously there is no way to isolate the origin of the change process; disclosure patterns and relationship changes are mutually transformative. All we know for certain is that self-disclosure is one important catalyst in relationship development and change. It is not the only factor, nor is it uniformly positive. Couples must learn to balance its potential for enrichment with its potential for destruction. The couple who do this well, moderating negative disclosure with positive, alternating intimate talk with social activity, will find the greatest benefits from disclosure over the life cycle of the relationship.

3

Gender

Ann, 28, lives in Los Angeles, while her friend from college, Elaine, lives in Philadelphia. They talk regularly on the phone. Ann says, "Elaine is a good sounding board when I need to talk to someone. Sometimes she just listens, and sometimes she gives me advice. If I can't decide what I am going to do about a problem, she offers me her opinion."

Carl, 18, is a senior enrolled in high school. He has two male friends, Woody and Josh. Recently Carl broke up with his girlfriend, and he has been depressed. However, he only joked about the breakup with Woody and Josh because he didn't want them to see how upset he was.

Tyrone's wife, Roz, has been sick for several years. Neighbors talk admiringly about how he has been a "pillar of strength" during this crisis. Tyrone is deeply worried about his wife's illness, but he keeps his feelings to himself. He thinks he has to be the strong one.

The contribution that gender plays in decisions governing self-disclosure has been debated for more than three decades. In 1971 Sidney Jourard suggested, on the one hand, that gender role expectations required men "to appear tough, objective, striving, achieving, unsentimental and emotionally unexpressive" (Jourard,

1971b, p. 35), demeanors that would inhibit self-disclosure for males. On the other hand, Jourard suggested that gender role expectations required women to be nurturant and comforting, demeanors that would increase self-disclosure for females.

In this chapter we examine the evidence about the impact of gender on self-disclosure in close relationships. In particular, we suggest how gender-related decisions about self-disclosure may reflect *subcultural differences between males and females* (Maccoby, 1990, 1991; Maltz & Borker, 1982; Tannen, 1986, 1990). Men raised in North American culture (emphasis on white, Protestant, northern European background) are more likely to believe that task accomplishment is an important goal and that emotional control is one general strategy for facilitating that goal. Women, however, are more likely to believe that social-emotional closeness is an important goal and that emotional expression is one general strategy for facilitating that goal. When differences in self-disclosure occur between males and females in close relationships, it may be due to differences in goals (e.g., "agentic," or task-oriented, for males, and "communal," or social-emotional, for females). Both sexes use communication to meet their goals but may assign different goals to the same situation.

The notion of subcultural differences between males and females will be useful in explaining when "misunderstandings" occur between males and females in cross-sex communication (Tannen, 1990). A source of conflict and confusion that may occur in cross-sex relationships that does not exist to the same degree in same-sex relationships is that males and females may assign different goals for the same situation (as noted above). For instance, in a stressful situation, women may see their primary goal as disclosing their feelings of vulnerability and providing emotional support, while men in the same situation may see their primary goal as presenting an image of composure, which may place barriers to emotional closeness.

The topics that we review include (a) what males and females talk about and prefer to talk about with relationship partners—particularly with same-sex friends, (b) gender effects on disclosure in dating and marital relationships, (c) how males may exceed females in self-disclosure in a first meeting when males want to take the initiative in beginning a relationship, (d) mechanisms that may account for gender differences in disclosure, and (e) how gender differences in disclosure (female preferences for disclosing feelings, male preferences for containing feelings) may affect success in coping with relationship problems and, in turn, may influence relationship satisfaction/dissatisfaction. Our discussion of these topics is framed within the cultural differences perspective, a view suggesting that gender-linked differences and preferences in self-disclosure can be understood if we think about men and women belonging to different subcultures. Men and women share similarities because they are part of a larger society, but some differences between them are due to living in and growing up in different subcultures.

A word of caution is advisable about our analysis of gender and self-disclosure. Although there may be differences in the average level of self-disclosure between males and females, there is also considerable overlap between the sexes in how much males and females self-disclose (Dindia & Allen, in press; Hill & Stull, 1987; Youniss & Smollar, 1985). What is most crucial is that gender-related differences and preferences in disclosure can have consequences for how well individuals maintain their close relationships and solve relationship problems.

Before reading on, the reader might consider filling out the self-disclosure questionnaire shown in Table 3.1. If possible, arrange for some other men and women to fill it out too so that it will be possible to test informally some predictions about the role of gender and self-disclosure in close relationships.

❧ Gender Effects on Self-Disclosure in Same-Sex Relationships

Male-female conversation is cross-cultural communication. Culture is simply a network of habits and patterns gleaned from past experience, and women and men have different past experiences. From the time they're born, . . . [women and men are] treated differently, talked to differently, and talk differently as a result. Boys and girls grow up in different worlds, even if they grow up in the same house. And as adults they travel in different worlds, reinforcing patterns established in childhood. These cultural differences include different expectations about the role of talk in relationships. (Tannen, 1986, p. 125)

Table 3.1 Are There Gender Differences in Self-Disclosure in Conversations Between Friends?

Instructions: Think of a close friend who is male and a close friend who is female. Indicate for the items below the extent to which you have disclosed to each person (from 0, which means that you haven't discussed this topic at all, to 4, which means that you have discussed this topic fully and completely).

1. My personal habits.
2. Things I have done which I feel guilty about.
3. Things I wouldn't do in public.
4. My deepest feelings.
5. What I like and dislike about myself.
6. What is important to me in life.
7. What makes me the person I am.
8. My worst fears.
9. Things I have done which I am proud of.
10. My close relationships with other people.

You can obtain your overall self-disclosure score for each target person by adding up the scores across the ten items. The higher the score, the more likely you have disclosed to the target person. If a large number of individuals such as a class filled out the questionnaire, it might be possible to test some questions about gender-related differences in self-disclosure. For instance, do women on the average disclose more than men, regardless of the target person? Do individuals disclose more to a female friend than to a male friend? Some research suggests that more self-disclosure occurs when one or both persons are females than when two males interact together. Do males disclose more to a female friend than to a male friend? Do women disclose at a relatively high level to both male and female friends? If men disclose less intimately than women do, would these differences in disclosure influence how well partners in a close relationship handle their relationship problems?

SOURCE: From "Openers: Individuals Who Elicit Intimate Self-Disclosure" by L. C. Miller, J. H. Berg, and R. L. Archer, 1983, *Journal of Personality and Social Psychology, 44*, p. 1236. Used by permission of Lynn Miller, Rick Archer, and the American Psychological Association.

Research by Caldwell and Peplau (1982) with unmarried college students illustrates how women place more emphasis on intimate communication in same-sex friendships than do men. No significant differences were found between men and women in the total number of friends or in the number of "casual," "good," or "intimate" friends that were reported. In addition, no difference was found in the number of hours that men and women spent with friends in a typical week. However, women reported getting together with a best friend "just to talk" more often than did men (this happened about three times per week for women and only about two times per week for men). Both men and women indicated that they wanted intimate friendships (defined as someone "with whom one can really communicate and in whom one can confide about feelings and personal problems" [p. 725]). But they differed in how they wanted to spend time with their friends. When given the choice between "doing some activity" or "just talking" with a same-sex friend, more women than men (57% vs. 16%) preferred just talking, whereas more men than women (84% vs. 43%) preferred doing some activity. When asked to indicate the topics they typically talked about with their same-sex friends, women were more than twice as likely to list personal topics such as feelings and problems. Women were also more likely than men to talk about other people.

Caldwell and Peplau (1982) also asked same-sex individuals to role-play a conversation in which one person called to congratulate the other on a recent success. The results indicated that women expressed more feelings and were more emotionally supportive than men. The women who role-played a successful person expressed twice as many feelings as the men, and the women who role-played the congratulating person made more supportive statements than the men.

Gender differences in self-disclosure also may occur among older same-sex friends. Middle-aged individuals (average age nearly 50 years) were asked by Aries and Johnson (1983) to complete a questionnaire about communication with "*one* person of your sex whom you consider to be your close friend" (p. 1186). Females, compared to males, reported talking more frequently with same-sex friends about sensitive topics such as personal problems, doubts and fears, family problems, and intimate relationships. Women also reported talking with their same-sex friends more often than men about less personal topics, including hobbies and shared activities. The only topic that men said they discussed more frequently was sports. Men also reported talking more "in-depth" about sports than did women.

A study of social interactions of senior college students by Wheeler, Reis, and Nezlek (1983), using the Rochester Interaction Record, provides additional data about females' and males' intimate communications with same-sex and opposite-sex friends. The participants in the study were asked to keep a record of every interaction with their friends and others that lasted 10 minutes or longer during a 2-week period. Subjects provided data on interaction measures such as intimacy, self-disclosure, and other-disclosure (how much the other person disclosed to them).

Males in Wheeler et al.'s (1983) study reported a lower level of intimacy, self-disclosure, and other-disclosure in same-sex interactions, as compared to females. In opposite-sex pairs, males and females did not differ on the intimacy and disclosure measure, and the pattern was the same as the female same-sex interactions. Wheeler et al. also tested whether the sex differences in interaction intimacy depended on the closeness of the relationship. Perhaps females have more intimate interactions in general, whereas males are intimate only with a best friend. The sex differences in the same-sex interactions were present, whether the other person was a "best friend" or a "friend." In opposite-sex interactions (boyfriend/girlfriend; opposite-sex, platonic best friend; and opposite-sex friend), however, no sex differences in self-disclosure, other-disclosure, or interaction intimacy were found.

As these studies show, the topic of disclosure and the person chosen as a recipient reveal some of the different preferences held by men and women. In particular, women talking to women disclose more on personal or sensitive topics, express more feelings, and are more emotionally supportive with each other. Men talking to men, other than about activities-related issues, tend to avoid self-disclosure.

Let us consider how same-sex differences in self-disclosure may reflect cultural differences between males and females, assuming that men and women grow up and live in different subcultures (Maccoby, 1990, 1991; Maltz & Borker, 1982; Tannen, 1986, 1990). On the one hand, as part of the social learning of sex roles, boys may be praised and rewarded for being self-assured, decisive, independent, rational, and not losing control in the face of crises. These qualities contribute to taking and exercising leadership in interpersonal situations. Girls, on the other hand, may be rewarded for being affectionate, sympathetic, understanding, and sensitive to the needs of others. These qualities, in turn, contribute to being nurturant and emotionally expressive in relationships. These gender differences in social learning may affect how much men and women value showing their feelings and emotions. Furthermore, from early childhood, males and females play and socialize primarily with same-sex peers. In same-sex peer relationships these behaviors are modeled and reinforced. Boys form hierarchies and compete for status and leadership; girls play in smaller groups and engage in more talk and more reciprocal interaction. Thus men and women emerge, especially in regard to peer relations, from different worlds. (For a critique of the notion that gender differences in communication reflect subcultural differences, see Henley & Kramarae, 1991).

✄ Gender Effects on Self-Disclosure in Dating and Marital Relationships

> Ben, 33, loves his wife, Melissa, for many reasons. One of the most important is that he feels comfortable talking to her about his problems and concerns. He said, "At first I only told her the good things and the successes of the day. Eventually I realized that if we were going to be close, I could tell her about the bad things and the failures as well. She could help me cope with them and not feel so bad. I am open with my wife in a way that the guys at work would never expect."

> Doris, 42, has several girlfriends at work and in her neighborhood with whom she feels comfortable talking about personal concerns. Her closest confidant, however, is her husband, Mark. She said, "I tell him everything important that is on my mind."

Subcultural differences between men and women may be a factor in understanding dating and marital relationships. However, a larger societal assumption of an "ethic of openness" may influence how much males and females disclose in opposite-sex relationships. Both males and females might be expected to disclose intimately to their opposite-sex partners in the development and maintenance of a close relationship. If this in-depth self-disclosure actually occurs, then males and females should be about equal in self-disclosure to their partner in a close, opposite-sex relationship (Rubin, Hill, Peplau, & Dunkel-Schetter, 1980).[1]

A study of dating couples, conducted by Rubin et al. (1980), provided support for the notion of an ethic of openness. Individuals were asked, via self-reports, how much they had disclosed to their partners. In summary across a number of topic areas, 58% of the women and 57% of the men indicated that they had disclosed "fully" to their partners. Across the total number of items in the questionnaire, no significant difference was found in self-disclosure between men and women.

The ethic of openness seemed to encourage a high level of disclosure by a majority of the dating couples. For instance, a female participant, Betsy, reported, "One really good thing from the beginning is that we had a relationship in which we could talk about everything, and if something bothers us we can talk about it" (Rubin et al., 1980, p. 314). Betsy's boyfriend, Ross, told her, "I'm never going to hide or hold things from you, . . . you are the person I'm going to be totally open with and I hope will be totally open with me" (p. 314). On the other hand, the difference in subcultural values for men and women regarding disclosure still was found in many couples. A woman interviewed for Rubin et al.'s (1980) study reported that it was easier for her than for her boyfriend to talk about worries and insecurities. She said, "I guess he feels that he shouldn't have any worries, or that if he doesn't talk about them, they won't be there" (p. 314).

Although males and females in close relationships may expect to be generally open with one another, gender-linked differences in self-disclosure may occur when couples experience stress. Gottlieb and Wagner (1991) conducted an interview study of married couples who had a seriously ill child (either juvenile diabetes or cystic fibrosis). The husbands and wives had different preferences about how to cope with the stressful event, a disparity that influenced how they communicated with one another. Husbands favored a rational approach to dealing with the child's illness. For instance, husbands would place pressures on the wife to act more maturely (e.g., "Grow up, you have a child with this disease and you're going to have to live with it"), to avoid anxiety-provoking communication (e.g., "Yeah, yeah, yeah, heard it all before"), or to encourage stoicism (e.g., "Oh, cut it out, stop that; how can you feel so sorry for yourself"; "You're overreacting and overdramatizing"). Husbands more often than wives focused on the need to concentrate on the child's health problems ("He wants more attention, you have to give him more attention"), but these comments were likely to be directive and hostile.

Wives, in sharp contrast, sought to have their husbands express feelings more openly (e.g., "Will you wake up! Will you cry, do something to show me that you care!") and a larger share of the burden of the child care (given that the wives usually spent more time taking care of the child). It was also noteworthy that wives, compared to husbands, were more likely to engage in coping techniques designed to protect or shelter the spouse from the full weight of events associated with the child's feelings. For instance, the wife, compared to the husband, was more likely to forewarn the spouse about a reversal in the child's health in order to give him a chance to anticipate what would be happening.

Over time, the wives' needs for emotional support often went unanswered because these needs were counter to the husbands' focus on managing the task demands associated with the child's illness, on denying feelings, or on acting stoically. Many wives sought emotional support from interactions with other parents in the community through local chapters of the Juvenile Diabetes Foundation and the Cystic Fibrosis Foundation. Or, as some wives reported, they adopted a stoical manner themselves and hid their emotions (at least in the husband's presence) in order to avoid losing his support.

It appeared in Gottlieb and Wagner's (1991) study that the larger societal norm of openness in self-disclosure for couples fits more closely with the woman's, not the man's, perspective and made her feel that her husband was being uncooperative. It might have been useful if the couples understood that they were operating under somewhat different rules about disclosure. The husbands' unwillingness to talk about their feelings may have reflected the male subcultural view that men are supposed to be "strong" and task oriented in managing family problems.

ᴥ Men Exercising Control in an Initial Acquaintance Situation: A Case Where Males May Exceed Females in Self-Disclosure

Debra met Gordon at a local club near the campus. Gordon asked her to dance, and later he joined Debra and her friends at their table. Debra and Gordon went out for breakfast after the club closed, and they talked most of the night away. He told her very personal things about himself and his family. Debra was surprised how quickly he opened up. But he seemed to have a lot to share and was interested in Debra's reactions and in what she said about herself too. They have been together several times since that night but never have been quite as open and revealing. Gordon seemed to set the pace that first night and she followed, but since then he has backed off talking about himself.

Our view of subcultural differences between males and females suggests that males, compared to females, value "taking control" and "being in charge." Hence, in the beginning of a relationship between a man and a woman, males might be more assertive than females and more likely to take the initiative. Men have been expected to start a conversation, issue a dinner invitation, and ask a woman for a date, as well as initiate physical contact and sexual intimacy (Green & Sandos, 1983; Huston & Ashmore, 1986; Peplau, Rubin, & Hill, 1977). If making verbal overtures is considered to be more appropriate for males than females, self-disclosure can provide men an opportunity to initiate and pace the start of an opposite-sex relationship. On the one hand, a man who is attracted to an opposite-sex partner might disclose more than the woman will. On the other hand, a woman who finds a man to be particularly attractive may not begin the social encounter by disclosing at a high level of intimacy for fear of being seen as taking the initiative.

A study by Davis (1978) illustrates how men and women may differ in self-disclosure when they first meet. Female and male college students took turns selecting what topics they would talk about in an acquaintance exercise with an opposite-sex partner. (The topics had been prescaled to represent low, medium, and high intimacy levels.) The results indicated that the men exercised more influence than the women in the selection of the level of topic intimacy in the conversations. The men selected more intimate topics to talk about than did the women, independent of their partner's choices and regardless of who went first. The women assumed a reactive role in that they tended to reciprocate the level of topic intimacy selected by their partner. The level of intimacy of self-disclosure by the men exceeded the level of intimacy of their partner, as well as the level of intimacy selected by the women who were assigned to same-sex dyads in the acquaintance exercise.

The males in Davis's (1978) study seemed to enjoy getting their female partner to increase her level of disclosure. The males' ratings of enjoyment in the opposite-sex encounters correlated positively with the level of intimacy of their female partner's disclosure, but the female's enjoyment of the encounters was not significantly correlated with the male partner's level of disclosure. The females enjoyed the acquaintance exercise most in same-sex dyads where intimacy of the topics selected was the lowest.

A follow-up investigation by Derlega, Winstead, Wong, and Hunter (1985) examined self-disclosure in an acquaintance exercise between all possible pairs of gender of discloser and gender of disclosure target. Groups of five to eight persons (about equally divided between males and females) met first for a short get-acquainted session. After the group conversation, subjects were individually assigned a bogus partner for the second phase of the session. For half of the subjects, one of the women from the group was identified as the partner; for the other half of the subjects, one of the men from the group was identified as the partner. Subjects were asked to prepare a self-description for the partner (which was used to measure disclosure intimacy), as well as to fill out a form concerning their perception of the partner.

The results were consistent with the prediction that men may exceed women in self-disclosure in order to control initial development of a cross-sex relationship. Males disclosed more intimately than females to the opposite-sex partner. Males paired with a female also exceeded the level of disclosure intimacy for females paired with a female or males paired with a male. For female subjects, their level of disclosure intimacy was quite similar with either a female or male partner.

The results from the studies conducted by Davis (1978) and Derlega et al. (1985) indicate the importance of the social context (Huston & Ashmore, 1986) in understanding gender-related patterns of self-disclosure. The value of control for males seems to influence their decisions to disclose. In an initial encounter, men may be less constrained than women in disclosing intimately to an opposite-sex partner with whom they are interested in developing a relationship. Males can use self-disclosure to cultivate a relationship with their female partner, a facility that reflects a traditional cultural view that males are supposed to make the first move in developing a male-female relationship. Females, on the other hand, may have more misgivings about being identified as the initiator of the relationship (see Abbey, 1982). Even when a woman is attracted to a man, she may avoid taking the initiative and let the man set the pace and level of intimacy in an initial social encounter.[2]

✥ Mechanisms Underlying Gender Differences in Self-Disclosure

Why do men frequently avoid disclosing their feelings, whereas women tend to express their emotions and feelings? We now consider how gender differences in self-disclosure may be due to:

1. The different value placed on self-disclosure in male and female subcultures. Females may value talking about feelings and personal concerns with a friend or relationship partner more than males do.
2. Gender-related social norms about appropriate self-disclosure for males and females (including with whom to talk, what topics are appropriate to talk about, and at what level of intimacy).
3. Different expectancies about self-disclosure for males and females. People may perceive that men are unwilling or less comfortable talking about personal feelings than are women. Hence people may be less willing to talk with men about personal topics, a reluctance that, in turn, might discourage men from talking intimately about themselves.

Different value placed on self-disclosure in female and male subcultures. One reason for sex differences in disclosure derives from the fact that females, beginning in childhood or early adolescence, enjoy intimate conversations more than males do. Youniss and Smollar (1985), in a series of studies on adolescent friendships, found that both male and female adolescents report enjoying activities that allowed them to be with their friends and away from the supervision of parents, such as going out with friends to movies, shopping malls, parties, or just hanging around or driving around together. However, a major difference between females and males was that more females than males enjoyed just talking together with their same-sex friends. On the other hand, males, compared to females, were more likely to indicate that they most enjoyed "recreational or sports activities" (e.g., riding bikes, playing cards) and activities involving drug and alcohol use (e.g., "getting high and drunk," "getting wasted") with their same-sex friends.

When Youniss and Smollar (1985) asked adolescents what were typical conversations with a close, same-sex friend, the findings were similar. Female adolescents were more likely than male adolescents to report that typical conversations with close friends involved intimate discussions (such as, "We talk about our personal development," "We talk about our problems in our families"). In contrast, male adolescents were more likely than female adolescents to report that typical conversations involved nonintimate discussion (e.g., about school or grades).

A majority (about 66%) of the females in Youniss and Smollar's research had close, same-sex friendships that involved personal and supportive discussions, while less than half of the males had this form of same-sex friendships. In fact, about 30% of the males had friendships in which they did not engage in personal discussions, and the same percentage of males would even say that they were unlikely to tell their true feelings to their male friend.

The findings by Youniss and Smollar (1985) indicate that, on the one hand, more adolescent females than adolescent males place a high value on self-disclosure, especially in same-sex interactions. On the other hand, many male adolescents distrust intimate disclosure in their same-sex interactions. A possible consequence for males in adult relationships is that they may choose a style of coping with interpersonal problems that avoids openness and intimacy in communication. Perhaps because of their adolescent experiences of being cautious and defensive in same-sex interactions, many males may be wary of talking freely about their feelings even when open communication might be beneficial (e.g., in coping with relationship problems or obtaining support to deal with stressful events).

As these findings indicate, men and women may have different values regarding disclosure. This inference extends to ideas about appropriate self-disclosure. If men and women have different views on when it is considered appropriate to disclose, they may judge each other by different standards.

Gender-related norms about appropriate self-disclosure for males and females. Because of cultural expectations about the male role (including the proscription that men must avoid anything "feminine"), males may be more concerned than females about the negative consequences of self-disclosure (Petronio & Martin, 1986; Thompson & Pleck, 1987). Males who accept traditional beliefs about the manly role (including appearing strong and self-confident, achieving status and success, displaying "no sissy stuff") may fear being rejected or ridiculed or may perceive themselves to be "out of role" if they disclose their vulnerabilities. Supporting this view, Derlega and Chaikin (1976) found that attributions of mental illness were based on the extent to which self-disclosure adhered to or deviated from the appropriate sex-stereotyped behavior for males and females. Both females and males rated a male stimulus person as being better adjusted psychologically when he failed to disclose about a personal problem to another person, but a female stimulus person was rated as better adjusted when she disclosed than when she did not disclose (also see Chelune, 1976; Snell, 1986; Snell, Miller, & Belk, 1988).

As adults, men also may learn in the workplace that it is inappropriate to display "negative" feelings that might suggest uncertainty, fear, or anxiety. Men are expected to act self-assured at work because the expression of emotions is interpreted as a sign of weakness or loss of control (Weiss, 1985, 1990). Commenting on problems that occupationally successful men have in discussing work and feelings with their wives, sociologist Robert Weiss (1985) noted how the necessity to control one's feelings at work may make it difficult for men to divulge their feelings at home:

> The world of work appears to support the practice of masking one's weaker emotions from others and from oneself as well. The man who appears to his wife to be emotionally unresponsive may in fact have many powerful, if conflicting, feelings but he may have schooled himself to keep his more suspect emotions under control. (Weiss, 1985, p. 57)

The expression of feelings of anger may be an exception to the rule that men should not display their feelings. A limited display of anger may be a good strategy for intimidating an opponent, in addition to serving to release pent up feelings. Weiss's (1985) study of middle-aged men in administrative or business-related positions found that showing anger in a situation that appeared to justify it was about the only expression of emotion that was considered to be acceptable.

Expectancies about gender differences in self-disclosure. The personal characteristics of males and females (e.g., how much they value self-disclosure) and norms about "appropriate" gender-related behavior may influence self-disclosure. However, people's expectations about how much a male or a female is interested in self-disclosure may affect behavior toward someone so that these beliefs (even if they are erroneous) subsequently are confirmed by the other's behavior (Deaux & Major, 1987; Merton, 1948; Snyder, Tanke, & Berscheid, 1977). For example, people may believe that women are more likely than men to enjoy intimate discussions, be more open in talking about their feelings, and show more interest and understanding in response to another's disclosure input (Derlega et al., 1985). Given these gender-linked beliefs that men are "less interested in self-disclosure," individuals may disclose more intimately to a woman than to a man, and the woman, in turn, may reciprocate with greater self-disclosure. In contrast, if people believe that men are more embarrassed and upset talking about intimate topics, they might avoid bringing up these topics in conversations with men who, in turn, are themselves nondisclosing.

A study by Chesler and Barbarin (1984) of parents whose children had cancer suggests how gender-linked expectancies about the male role may stand in the way of men expressing their emotional needs and receiving psychological support from their friends. The parents with seriously ill children often reported that they had available a family member or friend who served as a confidant or source of emotional support. However, mothers were more likely than fathers to have a confidant. Here is how one father described his difficulties in obtaining support:

> I think if I knew someone in my position one of the things I'd like to ask him is how are you coping. I did not experience that much, only a couple of people asked me how are you doing. I think my wife experienced that a lot with friends, but I only had a couple of friends who asked me. If I could wish for anything it would have been more of that. Probably there are things I could have done to make that happen though. (pp. 126-127)

Male friends in Chesler and Barbarin's (1984) study seemed to be particularly cautious in bringing up emotional issues when talking to the fathers, in part, due to their beliefs that the father would be uncomfortable with self-disclosure, advice giving, or sympathetic listening. One male friend wrote the following:

I would have liked to talk with him more about what was going on with him in terms of his thoughts and feelings. I didn't feel comfortable that he would have felt comfortable with me about those sorts of things. I felt a little helpless in that regard. (p. 127)

In Chesler and Barbarin's study, the image of males as strong or as unwilling to deal with their feelings made it more difficult for individuals to give emotional support to the fathers than to the mothers. If men and women are perceived differently, that may influence how others behave toward them and, in turn, how men and women react (also see Gottlieb & Wagner, 1991, discussed earlier). However, the extent to which gender-related expectancies about self-disclosure are confirmed also may depend on a prospective discloser's self-conception about how much men, as compared to women, can self-disclose. For instance, a male who is involved in a bitter divorce proceeding may believe that men are less able and comfortable self-disclosing personal feelings. This male may be less likely to seek out persons who are willing to listen. He also may be less relaxed talking about his difficulties; such unease, in turn, makes a listener uncomfortable. Thus expectancies generated by males or females themselves in the role of prospective discloser may influence how much they disclose.[3]

❧ Gender Differences in Self-Disclosure and Success in Coping With Relationship Problems

Because different subcultural orientations may influence judgments and subsequent behavior, success at maintaining a close relationship may be a challenge. In this section we consider how gender differences in self-disclosure influence couples' success in coping with relationship problems. If males and females generally differ in their willingness to self-disclose, do these gender-related patterns of self-disclosure affect relationship satisfaction? Research indicates that, for both males and females, self-disclosure about one's personal feelings and background—what usually is measured by paper-and-pencil self-disclosure scales (e.g., Jourard, 1971a; Miller, Berg, & Archer, 1983; Taylor & Altman, 1966a, 1966b)—is positively correlated with satisfaction in friendships, dating, and marital relationships (Hendrick, 1981; Hendrick, Hendrick, & Adler, 1988; Jones, 1991). Thus the ability to self-disclose about personal facts and feelings plays a key role in a successful relationship (Derlega & Margulis, 1982; Jones, 1991).

However, when stress and conflict are experienced in a personal relationship, partners may resort to gender-stereotyped modes of communication concerning their feelings about the relationship (e.g., the female talks about *her* negative feelings, but the male avoids talking about *his* feelings); such behavior contributes to misunderstandings and relationship dissatisfaction. Consider the following example of a couple having difficulty talking about a relationship problem:

> A husband is sitting in the living room; the television is on; Tom Brokaw is delivering the news; the husband is reading the sports page. The kids are quietly playing in the adjacent family room. The wife walks in, says hello, goes to touch base with the children, and then goes upstairs to change. Ten minutes later, she comes downstairs, approaches her husband and says, "We really need to talk." The husband doesn't answer. The wife says, "Harry, I said we really need to talk" (more emphatically and somewhat more negatively). The husband says, "Oh, were you talking to me?" The wife says, "You never listen to me; you never want to talk." The husband says, "That is not true, I love to talk; but we never talk, we just fight—just like this." The wife says, "There you go again, changing the subject on me. I really can't stand this much longer." The husband's veins pulse in his neck, and he switches his glare from his wife to the newspaper. The wife then gladly turns her attention to the increasing noise from the family room and goes to attend to the needs of the children. (Markman & Kraft, 1989, p. 51)

It is inevitable that couples will have relationship issues to confront, whether it is about money, sex, jealousy, housekeeping duties, leisure time, child care, in-laws, or disappointments (Huston, McHale, & Crouter, 1986). These difficulties may be aggravated, however, by females' expressions of negative feelings and males' withdrawal. For instance, a study by Kobak and Hazan (1991) found that the more wives expressed negative feelings during a problem-solving conversation (based on verbal and nonverbal communication rated as critical or rejecting by an observer), the less secure husbands felt about the relationship (describing the spouse as psychologically unavailable in satisfying their needs for comfort and support). On the other hand, the less the husbands were able to listen supportively during a disclosure exercise in which each person took turns talking about a personal disappointment or loss, the less secure the wives felt about the relationship. (Low listener support included interrupting the discloser by proposing solutions to the problem; high listener support included nonverbal and verbal cues that acknowledged the speaker's difficulties.)

The results in Kobak and Hazan's (1991) study may be understood in terms of the husbands' difficulties in providing responses based on the wives' disclosure input. A disclosure message may set up an expectation for a response by marital partners (Petronio, 1991). Given the nature of a marital relationship, partners count on each other to listen to or act on the information revealed. Perhaps the expression of negative feelings by the wife, especially if it was unsolicited, conveys a demand to the husband to be more responsive. The husband may not have been able to determine a satisfactory way to address this expectation. Thus the husbands in Kobak and Hazan's study may have felt less secure about the relationships and about their ability to meet the needs of their wives who expressed negative feelings.

When wives disclosed about a personal disappointment, they expected a listening, supportive response. When the husbands did not respond according to the implicitly communicated expectations, the wives deemed that the husbands were not fulfilling their marital obligation or responsibility to them, and the wives felt less secure about the relationship.

However, there may be an alternative explanation for Kobak and Hazan's (1991) findings. It might be that males in distressed marriages feel insecure about their marriage when the wife is verbally critical because males, compared to females, are uncomfortable and upset by their spouse's disclosure of feelings. In these circumstances, the males may feel less in control. Support for this view is based on physiological data demonstrating that males are more upset than females by their spouse's display of negative emotions. Notarius and Johnson (1982) arranged for married couples to engage in a problem-solving conversation about an important relationship issue. Skin conductance levels were recorded for each partner during the conversation. The husbands were found to have higher levels of skin conductance during the periods of time when they were "neutral" listeners (when they displayed no positive or negative affect themselves) than did the wives. These results support the view that males are more likely than females to be upset by their spouses' displays of negativity.

An effect of a husband's discomfort with negative emotions being expressed in the marital relationship is that he may stop attending to or understanding what his wife is communicating; such termination may worsen the marriage's problems. By doing so, he compromises his obligation to respond. For instance, in a study conducted by Gottman and Porterfield (1981), husbands and wives were told to communicate on a videotape recording a standardized statement, but the meaning of the message would depend on the style of delivery. The listener's task (either a spouse or a stranger) was to watch the videotape and decide which of three alternative messages was being conveyed. The results indicated that the couples' marital satisfaction was correlated with the husbands' but not the wives' ability to decode the spouse's message. The poor decoding performance of the distressed husbands was not due to their wives' poor "sending" ability, because male strangers had no trouble in decoding accurately the wives' messages. In addition, the distressed husbands' poor performance in correctly understanding the message that their wives attempted to convey was *relationship specific* because these men had no trouble in understanding correctly the message conveyed by women whom they did not know (Gottman & Porterfield, 1981; also see Notarius & Pellegrini, 1987).

In a conflict situation, females in a marital relationship may be more likely to express negative feelings, while the males may try to contain their own feelings and may be uncomfortable with or even unaware of their wives' feelings. A wife may escalate her expression of negativity because she experiences unresponsiveness by her husband, which may, in turn, lead the husband to try to control the wife's emotional display (e.g., telling her to "be rational" or "calm down"). Or the wife's negativity may lead the husband to withdraw further from the interaction, or his emotional control may lapse, in an extreme case, as he becomes "dramatically expressive" and cannot hold in his feelings anymore (Notarius & Johnson, 1982).

If couples are to resolve relationship problems, they must figure out ways of confronting conflict and negative feelings in their relationships. Although the expression of disagreement and criticism may be unpleasant and may make couples miserable in the short term, wives' and husbands' willingness to face the conflicts (by expressing disagreement and criticism, such as indicating disapproval of a certain behavior by the partner or using a hostile tone of voice) can produce marital satisfaction in the long run (see Gottman & Krokoff, 1989). Differences between how the sexes handle conflict and disagreements may push men and women away from one another emotionally. To achieve a satisfying relationship, however, couples must learn to talk about relationship issues in a context where both partners disclose their thoughts and feelings and where each perceives that he or she is understood and supported by the other (Gottman & Krokoff, 1989; Markman & Kraft, 1989).

⮞ Conclusions

As this chapter has suggested, there are two levels on which to understand gender and disclosure. The general cultural expectation is one of openness and sharing of personal information in close relationships. Both men and women are expected to disclose. The notion of subcultures of men and women, however, illuminates the gender differences in self-disclosure in same-sex friendships and the miscommunications between men and women in intimate relationships. Women hone their skills in self-disclosure and learn to trust the relationship-enhancing qualities of self-disclosure in their same-sex, peer relationships. Males, in peer relationships that emphasize competition and challenge, learn to avoid revealing weaknesses and may associate self-disclosure with loss of control and vulnerability. Thus males and females may not only reveal different preferences for and patterns of self-disclosure but also have different interpretations of the meaning and purpose of self-disclosure. Moving beyond the study of gender differences, researchers might examine male and female uses of self-disclosure.

A final comment about subcultural differences between women and men: Like all cultural identities, gender roles are not so much explicitly taught as they are "absorbed" from the personal and mediated messages received by children as they are growing up. Like all aspects of cultural identity, gender roles are not uniformly internalized by members of a culture. Some women and some men have internalized their gender role identity very strongly, whereas others have not; it may be only in the former group that gender has a strong effect on self-disclosure in close relationships.

❧ Notes

1. Although data are not available, in light of the idea of an "ethic of openness," gay males who are in homosexual, close relationships, as well as lesbian females, might not differ from heterosexual males and females in the level of self-disclosure to their partners.

2. This section has suggested one circumstance (a male is attracted to a female in an opposite-sex first encounter) in which males may exceed females in self-disclosure. However, the results of a recent meta-analysis by Dindia and Allen (in press) indicate that, in general, males and females do not report differences in self-disclosure to a stranger, and observational data indicate that females, compared to males, disclose more to strangers (K. Dindia, personal communication, September 24, 1991).

3. In fact, little evidence documents that males are less capable of producing intimate self-disclosure than are females. For instance, Reis, Senchak, and Solomon (1985) videotaped interactions that women and men had with a same-sex best friend while they were trying to have a "meaningful" conversation. The videotapes were viewed by judges who rated the intimacy of the conversations on dimensions such as "disclosure of personal thoughts and feelings," "intimacy of topic," and "general intimacy of the conversation." Using an overall intimacy index derived from judges' ratings, the authors found no gender differences in ratings of the overall intimacy of the conversations. Similar results have been reported by Derlega, Winstead, Wong, and Greenspan (1987).

4

Privacy Regulation and Vulnerability

I love my parents deeply. But I would never tell them that I had an abortion while I was in college. My parents have always supported me, but they also tend to idealize me. It would shatter their image of me if I told them about the abortion, and it would hurt me to hurt them. (A 28-year-old bank manager)

I feel real close to my girlfriend. We have been going out together for 5 months. We've talked about some pretty serious things. But I haven't been able to tell her about the car accident I caused several years ago where I hit a 7-year-old who had run into the street. If I keep this relationship going with her, I have to be honest enough to tell her what happened. (A 23-year-old college senior)

I told my boyfriend, Mike, what I felt was intimate material about my family. My dad had a drinking problem, and recently he became a patient in a drug rehabilitation program. Mike told me he knew I must love him because I could share this secret with him. The funny thing, though, is that I hardly see Mike anymore. He acts really "courteous" when I see him at school, but we haven't gone out together since I told him about my dad being an alcoholic. I guess there's someone out there whom I may meet that I can tell personal things to . . . but I haven't met him yet. (A 22-year-old college student)

These quotes illustrate the vulnerability and risk that individuals sometimes experience when they decide to disclose personal information. Although self-disclosure may contribute to one's self-worth by providing access to social support during stressful periods or by promoting the growth of close relationships, there is also the risk of being rejected or exploited by others. Thus people often have two competing needs that must be balanced: the need to share personal information and the need to preserve a sense of privacy. In this chapter we use a privacy regulation perspective (Altman, 1975; Derlega & Chaikin, 1977; Petronio, 1991) to describe the way in which individuals balance disclosure and privacy.

ᔐ Privacy Control Mechanisms

Arthur Ashe, 48, an African-American tennis star from the 1960s and 1970s, contracted the AIDS virus during a 1983 heart operation. He told only a few friends and family members that he was carrying the AIDS virus, and he asked them to keep this information a secret. However, he was recently forced to make a public announcement when a reporter for *USA Today* called to ask him to confirm or deny a tip about his condition. As Ashe said, "Someone just called [the newspaper] and ratted on me." (Winston, 1992, p. A1)

Seiji, a 22-year-old college student, wanted to share his concerns about what kind of career to pursue with his girlfriend, Yoko. However, he hesitated to talk about his worries because one of his past girlfriends had ridiculed him when he had disclosed similar concerns. Seiji figured that he would not say anything personal to Yoko until he felt he could trust her more.

The disclosure of personal information and feelings may create risks. If individuals know personal information about us, they may divulge this information to people we do not know or like; disclosers may find out that others avoid or do not like them after they talk about certain matters; individuals who disclose personal information with the notion of strengthening a close relationship may discover that the recipient of the disclosure is indifferent to the bid for intimacy or even may ridicule them.

British social psychologist Peter Kelvin (1977) eloquently described the risks of self-disclosure. He wrote, "The disclosure of areas of privacy reveals the underlying causes and motives of the individual's behavior: this potentially gives those to whom they are disclosed power over him [or her]; and in doing so, disclosures make him [or her] vulnerable to exploitation" (p. 15). Individuals may hold back personal information because they are afraid of what someone else will do with the information. On the other hand, self-disclosure depends on the perception that the information is safe when divulged to others.

In a privacy regulation model of self-disclosure, privacy represents control over the amount and kind of information exchange that persons have with one another. If individuals can voluntarily choose how much or how little information to divulge about themselves to another, privacy is maintained. If someone else can control how much information persons reveal about themselves or how the information is disseminated to others, then a lower level of privacy exists (Altman, Vinsel, & Brown, 1981; Burgoon et al., 1989; Derlega & Chaikin, 1977; Petronio, 1991).

It is useful to consider adjustments in self-disclosure outputs and inputs as similar to the opening and closing of "boundaries." Altman (1975), for instance, wrote:

> Privacy is conceived as an *interpersonal boundary process* by which a person or group regulates interaction with others. By altering the degree of openness of the self to others, a hypothetical personal boundary is more or less receptive to social interaction with others. Privacy is, therefore, a dynamic process involving selective control over a self-boundary either by an individual or by a group. (p. 6)

Self-disclosure contributes to the boundary regulation process. Adjustment in self-disclosure is an example of boundary regulation, and the more one has control over this information exchange, the greater the amount of privacy one has in a social relationship.

Although adjustments in self-disclosure represent a form of boundary regulation, it is useful to imagine two boundaries involved in self-disclosure (Derlega & Chaikin, 1977), as illustrated in Figure 4.1. One boundary, the *dyadic boundary,* is perceived by the individual as the boundary within which it is safe to disclose to the invited recipient and across which the self-disclosure will not pass; that is, the discloser believes that the disclosure is safe with the recipient.

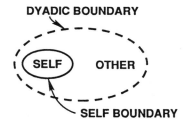

DYADIC BOUNDARY

NONDISCLOSURE: BASED ON A
CLOSED SELF BOUNDARY AND AN
OPEN DYADIC BOUNDARY

SELF BOUNDARY

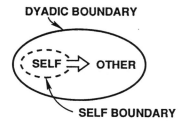

DYADIC BOUNDARY

SELF-DISCLOSURE: BASED ON
AN OPEN SELF BOUNDARY AND
A CLOSED DYADIC BOUNDARY

SELF BOUNDARY

Figure 4.1. Self-Disclosure as a Function of Self and Dyadic Boundary
Adjustments
SOURCE: From "Privacy and Self-Disclosure in Social Relationships" by V. J. Derlega and A. L.
Chaikin, 1977, *Journal of Social Issues*, 33(3), p. 105. Copyright © 1977 by the Society for the
Psychological Study of Social Issues. Reprinted by permission.

For instance, the expectation of confidentiality is an example of a
closed dyadic boundary where we expect that personal information
we reveal to a friend will not be passed along to mutual acquaintances. The dyadic boundary is perceived as open if we expect that
a friend will tell others information that supposedly is divulged in
confidence.[1] The second boundary, the *self* (or *personal*) *boundary*,
separates the discloser and his or her information from the recipient.
A closed self boundary means that information about oneself is
withheld or concealed from the other; an open self boundary means
that the information is shared.

An individual regulates the extent to which he or she is open
(discloses) or closed (avoids disclosure). The decision to self-disclose
(or open the self boundary) depends on the degree of risk that a
person perceives. According to Kelvin (1977), a person's *tolerance of
vulnerability* influences whether or not someone will divulge private

information. If the level of vulnerability is tolerable, then a person may adjust the self boundary to be open. If not, the self boundary remains closed, and information is not revealed.

Many factors contribute to the assessment of one's tolerance of vulnerability. Rawlins (1983) suggested, for example, that trust of the recipient is one way to judge risk. Perceived risks may vary, depending on whether the self boundary or the dyadic boundary is being controlled. In addition, individual differences affect perceived vulnerabilities associated with self-disclosure.

❧ Individual Differences in Perceived Vulnerability Associated With Self-Disclosure of Private Information

> Kim, an office manager at an accounting firm, does not believe that she can trust anyone at the office with private information about herself. She thinks that people at work gossip too much, and they are easily hurt if she says anything critical about them. Outside work, Kim has two very close friends. She trusts them because she thinks they can keep a secret and they don't get upset if Kim tells them what is on her mind—even if it may be somewhat critical of them.

In an extension of Kelvin's (1977) ideas on tolerance of vulnerability, Rawlins (1983) suggested four situations in which people balance revealing with concealing private information and, therefore, control both personal and dyadic boundaries. Rawlins stated that trust in the other person's discretion is a critical factor, and when there is a high level of trust in conjunction with a high need to be open (e.g., to "get something off their chest"), people tend to be very tolerant of possible vulnerabilities. However, if there is a high need to be open but a low trust in the other person's ability to be discreet, the person must judge whether it is a good idea to disclose. When there is a low desire to be open and a high trust of the receiver, the person may decide that revealing would enhance the relationship. Finally, when there is a low desire to be open and a low trust, concealing tends to be the outcome.

Rawlins (1983) also proposed that the likelihood of candor, reflecting a dilemma between a need to be honest in disclosing something to a relationship partner versus the need to exercise restraint, enters into the decision to disclose. When there is a high need to be honest and to express one's "true" feelings about a relationship-related matter and when restraint in discussing a topic is not a concern (meaning that the other person will not be upset if a certain topic is brought up), candor is likely. But if a high amount of restraint is appropriate and there is a low need to be honest about a topic, candor is less likely.

Dilemmas associated with tolerance of vulnerability and likelihood of candor are used by individuals to assess the risk of disclosure. The more risk, the tighter the boundaries are controlled. But as the work by Rawlins and Kelvin suggests, individuals may differ in their concerns about risks that lead to feeling rejected or exploited by divulging personal information. For instance, the questionnaire presented in Table 4.1 measures individual differences in the "perception of risks associated with intimacy" (Pilkington & Richardson, 1988). Items focus on the risks associated with getting close to someone, such as the fear of being hurt or one's hesitation about divulging personal information. Individuals who score high on the Risk in Intimacy Inventory report a smaller number of close friends, less likelihood of current involvement in a romantic relationship, lower trust in others, and more difficulty in confiding to someone whom they supposedly trust without fear of embarrassment (Pilkington & Richardson, 1988).

Pioneering research by Hazan and Shaver (1987) suggests that early childhood experiences in interacting with parents may affect one's fears about intimate relationships, as well as one's willingness to self-disclose to a relationship partner. Hazan and Shaver (1987) classified adults into three groups—secure, avoidant, and anxious/ ambivalent—based on expectations about relationships that were developed in early childhood. If parents were sensitive and attentive to their child's needs, then the individual would develop a "mental model" of relationships as secure and safe. If parents were insensitive to the child's needs, then the individual would develop a model of relationships as characterized by a lack of trust and a fear of closeness. If parents were inconsistent in meeting the child's needs, then the individual would develop a model of relationships as a source of anxiety, involving a struggle between getting close versus possibly losing one's relationship partner (Ainsworth, Blehar, Waters,

Table 4.1 Measuring Individual Differences in Perceptions of Risk in Intimacy

To complete the questionnaire, the respondent is asked how much he or she disagrees or agrees with each of the following statements. The following 6-point scale is used to make ratings: strongly disagree (1), moderately disagree (2), slightly disagree (3), slightly agree (4), moderately agree (5), strongly agree (6).

_____ 1. It is dangerous to get really close to people.
_____ 2. I prefer that people keep their distance from me.
_____ 3. I'm afraid to get really close to someone because I might get hurt.
_____ 4. At best, I can handle only one or two close friendships at a time.
_____ 5. I find it difficult to trust other people.
_____ 6. I avoid intimacy.
_____ 7. Being close to other people makes me afraid.
_____ 8. I'm hesitant to share personal information about myself.
_____ 9. Being close to people is a risky business.
_____10. The most important thing to consider in a relationship is whether I might get hurt.

NOTE: To determine someone's score, add the numbers given for each statement. The higher the score, the higher the perception of risk in intimacy.
SOURCE: Adapted from "Perceptions of Risk in Intimacy" by C. J. Pilkington and D. R. Richardson, 1988, *Journal of Social and Personal Relationships, 5*, p. 505. Copyright 1988 by Sage Publications Ltd. Adapted by permission of the authors and Sage Publications Ltd.

& Wall, 1978; Bowlby, 1969; Hazan & Shaver, 1987; Shaver, Hazan, & Bradshaw, 1988). These early attachment experiences provide the basis for personality styles in adulthood that, in turn, influence how individuals form affectional bonds and close relationships. For instance, securely attached persons believe that it is "easy to get close to others," and they are "comfortable depending on them and having them depend on me." Avoidant persons describe themselves as "uncomfortable being close to others," and they have difficulty trusting or depending on others. Anxious/ambivalent persons believe that "others are reluctant to get as close as I would like. I often worry that my partner doesn't really love me or doesn't want to stay with me" (Hazan & Shaver, 1987, p. 515).

The three attachment styles are related in adulthood to the love experiences reported by individuals. In survey studies conducted by Hazan and Shaver (1987), secure persons were most likely to report that they trusted, accepted, and felt friendship for someone who was their most important love relationship; avoidant persons' love relationships were characterized by a fear of closeness; and anxious/ambivalent persons' love was associated with being obsessed about the relationship, falling in love at first sight, and a desire for union ("a 'we' without clear boundaries") with the other person.

Research conducted by Mikulincer and Nachshon (1991, Study 3) provides information about how secure, anxious/ambivalent, and avoidant individuals differ in their willingness to self-disclose as a function of the level of disclosure input provided by another person (a confederate) in a study on how people get acquainted. The results indicated that the secure and anxious/ambivalent subjects were more intimate in their self-disclosure in response to a high versus low intimacy disclosure from another. The measure of self-disclosure, called *descriptive intimacy* (Morton, 1976, 1978), was based on a measure of willingness to reveal factual information about oneself. The avoidant subjects showed a low level of descriptive intimacy in both the high and low intimacy input conditions. In addition, secure and anxious/ambivalent subjects reported liking their partner more in the high intimacy input than in the low intimacy input condition, while avoidant subjects reported a low level of liking for their partner in both the low and high intimacy input conditions.

On a negative mood measure (based on how anxious and tense subjects felt), avoidant persons felt more upset, compared to secure and anxious/ambivalent persons, when talking with the high intimacy confederate. Negative mood scores were generally low and did not differ among the secure, anxious/ambivalent, and avoidant groups of subjects when talking with the low intimacy confederate.

The paper by Mikulincer and Nachshon (1991, Study 2) provides further evidence that avoidant individuals, compared to secure and anxious/ambivalent individuals, are more likely to avoid self-disclosure. Subjects were invited by telephone to be in a study on relationships. They expected to meet someone whom they did not know. Subjects in a "high disclosing partner" condition were told that their partner would be someone who liked to talk about themselves and to share personal thoughts and feelings with others. Subjects in a "low disclosing partner" condition were told that their partner did not like to talk about themselves or to share personal thoughts and feelings with others. Subjects were asked questions about their willingness to self-disclose to the partner, how they expected to feel during a conversation with the partner, and their liking for the partner.

Results showed that secure and anxious/ambivalent subjects were more willing to self-disclose to a high disclosing than a low disclosing partner, whereas avoidant subjects were generally unwilling to self-disclose to the high and low disclosing partners. Also, avoidant subjects expected to feel less comfortable, compared to the secure and anxious/ambivalent subjects, in a conversation with a high disclosing partner. The secure, anxious/ambivalent, and avoidant groups did not expect to feel uncomfortable in a conversation with a low disclosing partner.

On a measure of liking for the partner, secure and anxious/ambivalent subjects liked the high disclosing partner more than the low disclosing partner, whereas avoidant subjects did not differ in their liking for the high or low disclosing partner. Finally, secure and anxious/ambivalent subjects, compared to avoidant subjects, liked the high disclosing partner more.

Mikulincer and Nachshon's (1991) research illustrates how individuals with avoidant styles may be unwilling to self-disclose because they seek to prevent intimate social interactions. This research also suggests that individuals with an avoidant model of relationships may feel threatened and unsafe in the presence of a high disclosing partner. Avoidant individuals, besides avoiding self-disclosure, were uncomfortable interacting with a high disclosing partner. Low self-disclosure by avoidant persons provides a barrier to prevent a potentially threatening, intimate conversation from occurring.

❧ Secrets and Taboo Topics in Close Relationships

Harry works as a civilian, engineering consultant for the Navy in Norfolk, Virginia. He is married and has two children. He was sent to San Diego for 6 months to work on the design of a new ship for the Navy. When Harry went to San Diego, his family remained in Norfolk. He had an affair with a woman he met in San Diego, but he never told his wife what happened.

Wynne, a junior in college, never told her boyfriend, Morgan, about her previous intimate relationships. Wynne is the first person with whom Morgan has had a sexual relationship, and Wynne thinks that he would be upset if he knew about her other relationships.

When the perceived risks become too great and the tolerance for vulnerabilities exceeds an acceptable level, we keep information secret. The 19th-century sociologist Georg Simmel stated, "The secret contains a tension that is dissolved in the moment of its revelation. . . . [It] is surrounded by the possibility and temptation of betrayal; and the external danger of being discovered is interwoven with the internal danger, which is like the fascination of an abyss, of giving oneself away" (Simmel, 1950, pp. 333-334).

In examining what individuals may avoid disclosing to others, it is worthwhile to make a distinction between private information and secrets. The distinction rests on the degree of access others have to our personal information. *Private information* refers to material that others do not normally know about us (e.g., opinions, beliefs, and feelings about ourselves, social issues, or relationships with others) but that we might be willing to disclose based on others' need to know. "Private" information might be divulged if we wanted to develop a close relationship with someone, to obtain assistance in solving a personal problem, or to communicate concerns about a relationship-related problem. *Secrets*, however, refer to content that we actively withhold and conceal from others. "Secret" information might be disclosed under unusual conditions, but it often is concealed because the material is considered to be too threatening or shameful to divulge (e.g., a parent spent time in prison) or the disclosure of the secret would cause pain to oneself or others (e.g., to spare the children and themselves embarrassment, parents might not tell their children or neighbors that the father spent time in prison).

As Bok (1984) suggested, secrecy is intentional concealment. When we wish to keep secrets, we block others from obtaining the information by keeping it hidden from view. Because few people ever know our secrets, when we reveal them the recipient may gain power over us from the information obtained (Bok, 1984). But to know a secret also means that the receiver is burdened with the responsibility of the information. In close relationships some topics may be considered taboo because they either give too much access to the partner or burden the partner with the responsibility of the information. For instance, a woman might hesitate to tell friends that her husband is dying from cancer, because of her concern about imposing burdens on them; a husband might not tell his wife about prior sexual relationships to protect himself from embarrassment or to keep his wife from being upset with him; or parents might not tell their children about financial difficulties to spare them from worrying.

Research by Baxter and Wilmot (1985) indicates that individuals perceive certain topics as off-limits to talk about in an opposite-sex relationship. Baxter and Wilmot interviewed persons who were involved in opposite-sex relationships. Some relationships were platonic friendships; there was no sexual relationship or romantic attraction between the partners. Some relationships were high in romantic potential; the partners were more than "just friends" but did not define themselves as involved in a romantic relationship. Others were romantic relationships; both partners agreed that they were involved in a romantic relationship.

Participants in the study were asked whether they considered any topics to be taboo or off-limits in their conversations. From interviews with 40 males and 50 females, 172 taboo topics were generated, which fell into six major categories: (a) the state of the relationship between the partners; (b) extra-relationship activity, dealing with activities and social relationships outside of the relationship between the partners; (c) relationship norms or rules of behavior in the relationship, such as how the partners should treat one another; (d) prior relationships with persons of the opposite sex; (e) conflict-inducing topics, such as differences or dissimilarities between the relationship partners on various issues such as politics, religion, or attitudes about one's parents; and (f) negatively valanced self-disclosures, representing topics that might be damaging to one's self-esteem or unpleasant to talk about.

It will be of interest to examine the reasons given by Baxter and Wilmot's (1985) subjects for not talking about the "state of the relationship" and "extra-relationship activity," the two most frequently cited taboo topics in their study.

The state of the relationship. The state of the relationship was mentioned as a taboo topic mainly out of fear that such talk would undermine the relationship. Subjects perceived that talking about an unequal commitment to the relationship, for instance, would have the effect of destroying the relationship:

> For me right now, there's no way I'll get married, but sometimes I think he's more serious. . . . It's a sore subject and it makes me feel on the defensive (Baxter & Wilmot, 1985, pp. 259-260).

> It's hard to talk about what's going to happen in the future in the relationship. He knows more what he wants and I just don't know. Like if people ask me out, I want to go out with them to see if he's really the one. . . . I couldn't tell him this. I'm afraid of hurting and upsetting him. (Baxter & Wilmot, 1985, p. 260)

Another reason why the state of the relationship was not discussed was "individual vulnerability," or a threat to one's self-esteem. For instance, a male reported that:

> The relationship itself [is a taboo]. I just never talk about those kinds of things. Never. Big mistake. Actually the only time I talk about those kinds of things is when I'm really drunk . . . 'cause then I don't care [what I find out]. It's a big mistake to talk about it because you leave yourself very vulnerable, which I don't like to be—your feelings can get hurt. (Baxter & Wilmot, 1985, p. 261)

Some individuals felt that talking about the relationship should be avoided in favor of a form of "tacit communication" in which the partners "just understood" one another. A male participant in the study said:

> Most of what I learned about the relationship wasn't from talking but from . . . being more perceptive. Understanding without being said. When feelings are involved, people won't lie but they may say things they don't mean. . . . [It helps] to let it be more natural. (Baxter & Wilmot, 1985, p. 261)

Extra-relationship activity. Several reasons were offered for not talking about one's own or the partner's other relationships. There was concern about "negative relationship implications" (e.g., jealousy and anger) if what might have happened outside of the current relationship were discussed. A woman said:

> I spent the summer in Guatemala and met this guy there. I write to him regularly, but I wouldn't tell this to my boyfriend because I don't want to hurt him. He's the all or nothing sort of person. It is all him or nothing. I don't want to make waves. (Baxter & Wilmot, 1985, p. 262)

The "right" to privacy was mentioned occasionally to justify avoiding talk of activities outside of the relationship. Persons believed that they and/or their partner had a right to privacy. A female mentioned this reason to explain why she did not talk about certain topics with a platonic male friend who was dating her girlfriend:

> There are some things there's no reason for the other to know. When he was going out with my friend no one in the dorm knew. He never talked about it and I never asked. It was none of my business. (Baxter & Wilmot, 1985, p. 262)

Concern about placing oneself between one's relationship partner and another person was cited as another reason for avoiding talk about other relationships. For instance, a male gave the following reason for not talking to a platonic female friend about certain conversations he has had with her boyfriend, who is also his friend:

> We don't talk about things that her boyfriend tells me about their relationship because she feels that this isn't right, that this would be destroying my friendship with her boyfriend. We both know that I shouldn't talk about stuff that her boyfriend says to me in confidence. (Baxter & Wilmot, 1985, p. 262)

Frequency of taboo topics in relationships. Baxter and Wilmot (1985) noted that all but three participants in their interview study of college students' opposite-sex relationships could identify at least one taboo topic that was off-limits for the relationship partners; avoiding explicit talk about the state of the relationship was the most frequently cited taboo topic. Although we generally associate increased openness with greater relationship closeness, talking explicitly about relationship issues was considered, according to Baxter and Wilmot (1985), "a destructive relational force" (p. 265). Perhaps because of a relationship's fragility, uncertainties about how a relationship was developing, or an individual's own uncertainties about being hurt if feelings for the partner are not reciprocated, relationship talk may be perceived as threatening and hence avoided. For instance, relationship talk was most likely to be avoided by "romantic potential" couples, whose relationships are in transition between being more than just friends but not yet being involved in a serious romantic relationship. The transition from one relationship to a more intimate relationship may connote uncertainty for the relationship partners, and they may be unwilling to risk the negative consequences that go along with relationship talk (Baxter & Wilmot, 1985; see also Metts, 1989).

Although explicit talk about the state of the relationship was the most frequently cited taboo topic, other taboo topics in Baxter and Wilmot's (1985) study touched on relationship issues that couples might wish to avoid. The taboo topics of extra-relationship activity and prior relationships raise questions about one's commitment to the relationship; relationship norms deal with rules about how partners should behave towards one another; and conflict-inducing topics imply that the partners are not compatible. In addition, avoiding disclosure of information that the other partner might consider as negative creates a false impression that might keep the relationship from breaking up.

Although Baxter and Wilmot's (1985) research documents the existence of taboo topics, their results do not answer the question whether keeping certain topics off-limits contributes to relationship satisfaction. When couples define some information as off-limits, they may do so to protect one partner or themselves. They regulate their privacy boundary by restricting access; however, this decision may have a positive or negative impact on the nature of the relationship.

Recent studies by Vangelisti (1991) provide evidence about the effects of keeping secrets on family functioning. The research focused on secrets that a family as a group tends to keep from outsiders, secrets that some members of a family kept from other members, and secrets that individuals kept from other members of the family. The results showed that the perceived number of secrets a family holds is negatively related to members' satisfaction with their family, and keeping family secrets is seen as providing a protective function. Keeping secrets in families may not necessarily be seen as a way to form bonds among the members but may function to protect them against possible risks of exposure to outsiders. Although keeping secrets may not lead to feelings of satisfaction with family relationships, it may reduce feelings of risk and vulnerability from those outside the family.

Disclosing Secrets to a Relationship Partner

Richard, 31, has recently enrolled for classes at a state university. He had spent 4 years in prison for committing an armed robbery, and he now is trying to put his life back together. He met Robin, a 22-year-old junior at the university, whom he likes very much. Richard wants to ask Robin to go out on a date with him, but he is not sure if he should tell her that he has been in prison.

Stanley had been gambling heavily for several months. He also had borrowed money so that his wife, Susan, would not know that he was spending almost his entire paycheck. Susan began to notice that $50 and $100, which they didn't have to spare, was disappearing from his weekly paychecks, evidently to pay back the money he had borrowed. When she questioned him, he confessed. He said he had borrowed the money to hide the fact that he had lost money while gambling. Susan told Stanley that because he had lied to her, she couldn't respect or trust him anymore.

Partners in a close relationship may declare certain topics (e.g., other relationships) as off-limits to talk about out of fear of jeopardizing the relationship, or someone who is trying to make new friends may conceal "negative" information about his or her past (e.g., being an ex-convict or former mental patient) or present (e.g., having herpes) to avoid rejection. Despite the tendency to conceal sensitive information, individuals in close relationships have strong expectations that their partners will be honest and that little deception will occur in their relationships (McCornack & Parks, 1986; Miller, Mongeau, & Sleight, 1986; Rubin et al., 1980). As Miller et al. (1986) noted, individuals in close relationships "are likely to operate from a strong *truth bias* in their communicative exchanges; i.e., they will probably assume veracity on their partners' parts unless presented with considerable conflicting evidence" (p. 509). In this section we consider when individuals might reveal potentially negative, personal information to a relationship partner, based on the partner's need to know, timing considerations, and the joint negotiation of the discloser and disclosure recipient.

The need to know: Disclosing content that is relevant to the relationship. It would be oversimplifying to assert that all personal information and feelings about oneself need to be disclosed to the relationship partner. During the 1960s, when the human potential movement was popular, there was almost a "cult of compulsive honesty." This view, in its extreme version, held that partners should disclose everything about themselves to the relationship partner. Compulsive disclosure can have a disastrous effect, particularly if it serves to sanction cruel and malicious behavior (e.g., saying sarcastically, "I have been having an affair for years, and you knew it!"). On the other hand, the opposite view is that "What he doesn't know won't hurt him." This attitude of "cavalier deception" (Karpel, 1980) rationalizes that concealing certain information from the relationship partner is in the other's best interest.

Individuals may be reluctant to divulge certain personal information or feelings about the relationship, perhaps to guard against being rejected by the partner or to avoid having to face relationship problems. In the best interests of a relationship, however, it might be appropriate to divulge information that affects issues of trust, trustworthiness, and caring for one's partner (e.g., disclosing to a spouse about having had an extramarital affair). On the other hand, it might not be necessary to disclose to a relationship partner about, say, having had a traumatic experience in one's childhood if the trauma has been reasonably resolved and there are no significant effects of the trauma on how the individual behaves in the relationship. Although the person who experienced the trauma may divulge the information to the relationship partner as a sign of trust and to give the other an accurate view of his or her life experiences, the information may not have to be shared with the partner if it does not have important implications for the relationship (Karpel, 1980).[2]

Timing in the disclosure of threatening information. If a person possesses negative information, what is the most appropriate time to divulge this information? Research suggests that to earn a favorable evaluation from a disclosure recipient, it is best to disclose negative information early in an interaction—particularly when the discloser is personally responsible for the negative event.

Consider the following study conducted by Jones and Gordon (1972). Subjects listened to a supposed interview between a student and his academic advisor. In some conditions the student has had some bad fortune—he had to miss a semester of high school because of litigation associated with his parents' divorce. The description of missing school because of the parents' divorce was the "no responsibility" condition. In a "responsibility" condition describing a negative experience, the student said he missed a semester of high school because he was expelled from school for cheating and plagiarism. The timing of the disclosure was manipulated by having the student volunteer the information either during an early segment of the interview with the advisor or in a later segment of the interview, after being asked a direct question about why he transferred high schools.

On the one hand, the student who was responsible for a negative event (cheating and plagiarism) was liked more when he revealed this information earlier in the interview, compared to later in the interview, when he had to "give up" the information in response to a direct question. On the other hand, the student who was not responsible for a negative event (transferring schools because of the parents' divorce) was liked less when he revealed this information early in the interview. The timing variable in Jones and Gordon's study, involving whether negative information was shared early or late in an interview, more precisely focuses on the discloser's eagerness or reluctance to disclose. (The timing variable was achieved by a combination of timing and whether the information was volunteered or provided as a response to a direct question.) On the one hand, reluctance to reveal information seemed to reinforce subjects' impressions that the cheater was untrustworthy because he possibly was trying to establish a relationship with his advisor under false pretenses. On the other hand, the student who was reluctant to reveal information about a negative event that he was not responsible for may have earned high marks because subjects believed he was not trying to gain sympathy.

A follow-up study by Archer and Burleson (1980) provides additional evidence that the timing of the disclosure about a negative event affects liking for the discloser. Subjects participated in a conversation exercise in which a confederate revealed either early or late in the interaction that his girlfriend had gotten pregnant. In a "choice" condition, the confederate supposedly arranged voluntarily the order of questions he was scheduled to answer. In a "no choice" condition, the confederate did not have the opportunity to arrange the questions in the order he preferred. The results indicated that, in the choice condition but not in the no choice condition, there was greater attraction (based on such questions as "How much do you like your partner?" "Would you like to have your partner as a close friend?") for the confederate who disclosed early compared to late in the conversation that his girlfriend was pregnant. In addition, subjects who heard the disclosure of the girlfriend's pregnancy early in the conversation by someone who voluntarily chose to do so were more likely to perceive that this was due to the confederate's feelings about the subject than about the discloser's basic personality. The subjects may have reasoned: "If the discloser wants to tell me early in a conversation about a negative event he was responsible for, his idea must be to start the relationship on an honest basis. On the other hand, if the discloser wants to avoid telling me until near the end of the conversation about a negative event, perhaps he is trying to hide the information or mislead me about what he is like."

The research by Jones and Gordon (1972) and Archer and Burleson (1980) suggests that individuals who do not previously know the discloser prefer the early disclosure of "negative" information about the self when the revealer is responsible for what has happened.[3] However, it is not inevitable that someone who has concealed something or has misled a partner will be rejected or the relationship terminated if the information is discovered. If the recipient of the previously hidden information infers that the discloser has good intentions in withholding the information (e.g., concern that divulging embarrassing information could hurt the relationship partner), then mutual trust might still be maintained.

Besides timing of the disclosure, on occasion an individual may wish to tell private information but feels the need to continue control over the disclosure. One of the issues of telling private information to someone is the possible further dissemination of that information to a third party. To indicate how seriously a person feels about the information disclosed, he or she sometimes may use a "prior restraint phrase" such as "don't tell anybody this, but" (Petronio & Bantz, in press). This kind of phrase sets the parameters for who else should know what is being disclosed.

Petronio and Bantz (in press) conducted a study to examine the extent to which this type of linguistic tool (prior restraint phrase) is useful in curbing subsequent dissemination of the discloser's private information. In one condition, respondents were asked to imagine that they disclosed slightly or moderately private information to a close friend and then to predict whether that friend subsequently would reveal the information to others. In the second condition, respondents were asked to imagine that they were the disclosure recipients of the private information that had been divulged and then to predict whether they would disseminate disclosed information from their close friend to others.

Results showed that a substantial percentage of both disclosers and receivers of private information expected recipients to pass on all levels of private information even when using a prior restraint phrase like "don't tell anybody." However, the subjects in the study expected that the third parties selected would be trusted friends or family members. Hence a prior restraint phrase may not stop the dissemination of private information, but it signals the need for discretion in selecting persons to whom the vulnerable and compromising information is passed along.

Couple-based strategies for managing the disclosure of vulnerable information. We have described how decisions to disclose negative information are based, in part, on disclosers' perceptions of the needs of the relationship and timing considerations within a conversation. It is worthwhile noting, however, that decisions to disclose negative information are not made *exclusively* by the possessor of vulnerable information. Particularly in a close relationship, partners are likely to coordinate their social interactions to enable the discloser to divulge vulnerable information without being personally embarrassed or threatening the disclosure recipient or the relationship itself. For instance, Holtgraves (1990) and Petronio (1991) noted how "indirect disclosures" might be used by a relationship partner to communicate feelings of vulnerability. Such disclosures are metamessages that tell the recipient something about the way the disclosing partner expects him or her to respond. For instance, a husband who feels humiliated because he was ridiculed by a supervisor at work may hint at problems to his wife by saying, "I feel like I have a lot on my mind; is it OK if we don't visit your parents this weekend?" The wife, recognizing that the husband is distressed, may reply that a change in their plans for the weekend is not a problem. But she might ask him, "Is there anything more that you want to talk about?" which gives the husband an opportunity to disclose more information if he wishes.

The person disclosing and the recipient of that private information often must mutually manage how, if, and when to disclose vulnerable information. Both relationship partners may be threatened if one of them mentions "out of the blue" (Holtgraves, 1990) a personal or relationship problem. Unsolicited disclosure (Gilbert, 1977) may negatively influence a person's feelings of self-esteem and may place relational partners in a position where they are expected to respond even if it causes stress or decreases satisfaction with the relationship. It also can be threatening if someone demands that the partner tell him or her directly what is wrong. Individuals need to devise strategies for disclosure so that their conversations do not threaten either the discloser or the disclosure recipient with embarrassment or loss of self-esteem, while also serving to coax out important information that affects the relationship. In essence, partners must balance the competing needs of maintaining relationship intimacy versus preserving their personal autonomy. Partners depend on criteria or rules to judge how to balance these needs. Sometimes the decisions have to do with the timing of the disclosure; sometimes individuals reveal information because they like the other; and sometimes individuals focus on whether the person receiving the private information is an appropriate or inappropriate target for disclosure.

❧ Choosing an "Appropriate" Versus an "Inappropriate" Disclosure Recipient

> Joe feels lucky about the relationship that he has with his wife, Barbara. He believes that he can tell her almost anything about himself without having to worry about whom she will talk to. He has never known a time when he told her something in confidence that she then told to members of their family or to friends living in their neighborhood.

> Mrs. Rojas considers her teenage daughter, Maria, to be her closest confidante. She tells Maria many things about herself that she does not even tell her husband. Mrs. Rojas thinks of herself as being loyal to her husband, but her husband thinks that she and Maria have formed an alliance that excludes him.

One can lose privacy by choosing an "inappropriate" recipient, such as someone who shares your secret with people with whom you do not want your secret shared or who uses the disclosures against you. By contrast, one can preserve the privacy of disclosures if information is shared with an "appropriate" disclosure recipient, who will protect the information.

The appropriateness of a recipient—based on the need to protect privacy—highlights a paradox of intimacy. To create intimacy, one must self-disclose, which, in turn, makes one vulnerable. However, an appropriate recipient will protect the discloser and his or her secrets. By knowing the discloser's secrets, the recipient knows the discloser's weaknesses and hence knows precisely what to protect (Kelvin, 1977). By contrast, an inappropriate recipient can create costly consequences for the discloser by abusing the trust, for example, by gossiping about what was said in order to deceive or exploit the discloser.

Individuals might be *appropriate* as disclosure recipients because of their acceptance of the discloser, skill in understanding the discloser's message, motivation to help, and discretion (willingness to restrict access to and protect disclosures revealed in confidence) (see Kelvin, 1977; Petronio, 1991; Westin, 1967). However, some individuals might be *inappropriate* as disclosure targets, not because they are indiscreet or untrustworthy, but because the nature of the social relationship between the discloser and the recipient creates complications.

For instance, a parent who considers a child to be a confidant and who also conceals the information from a spouse may create tensions for the entire family unit (Minuchin, 1974; Rohrbaugh & Peterson, 1986).

Family therapist Evan Coopersmith (1985) developed an exercise illustrating the possible strain on families when a parent shares a secret with a child but this "secret" is concealed from the other parent. Individuals are asked to play the roles of mother, father, and daughter in three types of families that are planning an outing. In Family 1, the mother and daughter create an overt alliance, based on common interests, that leaves out the father. In Family 2, the mother and daughter create a covert coalition against the father. In Family 3, each parent creates a covert coalition with the daughter against the other parent. Coopersmith found that Family 1 is able to plan the outing, but the father feels left out and jealous. The father wants to spend more time with his wife, while the daughter feels "privileged" because of her special relationship with her mother. Family 2 has difficulty planning because so much time and energy are spent guarding the secret relationship. Tension and stress are apparent (e.g., "I would go [on the outing] if I could, but my stomach hurts"). Family 3 also has difficulty planning for the outing. All family members, particularly the child who must be loyal to each parent, experience high levels of distress.

Coopersmith's (1985) findings do not mean that all disclosures between parent and child will be dysfunctional for their family. Rather, difficulties are likely to occur when disclosures by a parent to a child or by a child to a parent are considered to be "secret" and attempts are made to conceal or mislead the other family members about the true situation.

❧ Conclusions

We have shown in this chapter that a tension exists between disclosure and privacy. We need to be open at times, such as when we are under stress, and at other times we need to maintain our privacy. This duality represents a regulation process using a metaphorical boundary to control when we wish to reveal and when it is important to conceal. The maintenance of a privacy boundary allows us to preserve a sense of autonomy and individual identity. Regulating this boundary to be open is done under certain circumstances, such as when the timing is right, when we feel secure, and when the information is relevant to the recipient. These conditions are important because revealing ourselves makes us vulnerable. We risk giving information that may jeopardize our relations or compromise another's view of who we are. When the risk is high, as with secrets, we conceal this information unless unusual circumstances justify disclosing it.

Although self-disclosure about sensitive topics may impose risks, sharing this information with an appropriate disclosure recipient can be beneficial. The recipient of sensitive information who cares for us is in a better position to protect us than if he or she did not know what we were trying to keep hidden.

A final comment about privacy regulation in a close relationship: We have discussed how individuals experience risk associated with their self-disclosure and how this experience affects who is chosen as an appropriate disclosure target and what topic areas are selected for disclosure. In a close relationship, however, the risks of self-disclosure are often jointly shared because the relationship itself may be threatened if the information is disclosed inappropriately. Hence both partners in a committed relationship must negotiate how, when, and where to disclose sensitive content.

❧ Notes

1. Two possible infringements on privacy are represented by an open dyadic boundary. These are *violations of privacy* (e.g., a disclosure recipient tells others information that was divulged in confidence) and *invasions of privacy* (e.g., someone listens without permission to a supposedly private conversation).

2. Our discussion has emphasized how openness about relationship-related matters affects the ability of couples to get along with one another. However, empirical research is needed on the effects of being honest versus withholding (and even distorting or falsifying information) on relationship satisfaction. Metts (1989), for instance, found that the reasons given for deception in close relationships (including dating, engaged and married relationships, and friendships) influenced partners' satisfaction with the relationship. Individuals who justified deception in their relationship because of concern for partner (e.g., "I knew he would be terribly hurt if I told him," "I felt she couldn't take the truth at that time because she was so tired and

under so much stress") were more satisfied, felt closer to their partner, and perceived more commitment from their partner than those who justified deception based on a concern for self, relationship-focused, or issue-focused reasons.

3. Research by Jones and Gordon (1972) and Archer and Burleson (1980) examined the effects of timing of self-disclosure in a conversation between individuals who were not previously acquainted with one another. It is important to generalize these results to individuals who are already in a close relationship and choose to divulge negative information about themselves at different points in the relationship's history.

5

Coping With Stress and Social Support

This chapter focuses on *stress-reducing disclosure:* how people who are faced with upsetting life events are helped by talking with someone about what happened. Consider the following examples.

In March and April of 1979 a nuclear accident occurred at the Three Mile Island (TMI) Nuclear Power Plant in Pennsylvania. About 400,000 gallons of water were contaminated, and radioactive krypton gas was trapped in the containment building surrounding the reactor. The gas and water became sources of radiation exposure. A long period of uncertainty followed about how much radiation had been released and how damaging the consequences might be. About a year and a half after the accident, Fleming, Baum, Gisriel, and Gatchel (1982) conducted a study of residents who lived within 5 miles of the TMI nuclear power station. Results indicated that TMI residents experienced greater stress, compared to control subjects (those who lived within 5 miles of an undamaged nuclear or coal-fired power plant or far away from any type of power plant). TMI residents were more likely to complain about having physical symptoms (such as headache and nausea) and mood disturbances (such as depression, anxiety, and alienation). Biochemical measures of stress indicated that TMI residents exhibited higher levels of catecholamines (epinephrine and norepinephrine) in their urine.

Vulnerability to stress was not equal among all TMI residents. Persons who were least likely to have a confidant (based on a 6-item scale of availability of confiding relationships) reported a greater number of physical and psychological complaints than did TMI residents who were moderate or high in likelihood of having a confidant. Having a confidant did not influence catecholamine levels among the TMI residents. Thus, on self-report measures of physical and psychological functioning, having a confidant improved coping with the stressful event represented by the TMI disaster (Fleming et al., 1982).

In a survey conducted by Pennebaker and O'Heeron (1984), individuals whose spouse had died due to suicide or a motor vehicle accident were asked about their health and coping a year after the spouse's death. The purpose of the research was to examine how confiding in others might reduce health problems associated with a spouse's death. Subjects were asked how much they had talked about their spouse's death with close friends. They also completed a questionnaire assessing health problems they had in the year before the death of the spouse and in the year since the death. People experienced an overall increase in health problems in the year after the spouse's death, as compared with the preceding year. But the more time that individuals spent talking with someone about what happened, the less likely they were to experience increased health problems.

Individuals in Pennebaker and O'Heeron's (1984) study also answered questions about their continued thoughts about the spouse's death (e.g., "the degree to which they had been able to put the death out of their mind" and "the degree to which they constantly thought about the spouse's death"). After controlling for number of friends, subjects who talked more with friends were less likely to ponder the spouse's death. Pennebaker and O'Heeron speculated that the inability to confide may increase unwanted thoughts about the sudden death of the spouse, whereas confiding to the friend about what happened may reduce such thoughts.

These studies illustrate how people cope more successfully with stressful events when they have someone with whom to discuss their problems. Although illness and psychological problems may arise as a result of stress (Selye, 1976), we describe in this chapter how self-disclosure of major traumas can reduce the negative health consequences. In examining the linkage between self-disclosure and coping with stress, four topics are treated: First, we summarize studies documenting the linkage between disclosure/nondisclosure about a stressful life event and health outcomes. Second, we describe why disclosing to someone about stressful life events has positive effects for health and why failing to disclose has negative effects. Third, we examine situations in which self-disclosure about stressful events may not be beneficial. Fourth, we explore the issue of how many confidants should be available in order for someone to experience the benefits of self-disclosing.

ਏ The Linkage Between Confiding/Nonconfiding and Health

Heidi is 18 years old, and she has just enrolled as a freshman at a local college. When she was a child, Heidi's family spent 2 weeks each summer visiting her mother's brother. When this uncle kissed Heidi good night, he would stay in her bedroom and fondle her. Heidi never told anyone what happened, and she still feels confused and upset thinking about it.

Sheldon, 50, is a medical technician. Sheldon's mother died when he was 8 years old. Tears well up in Sheldon's eyes when he thinks about her. But Sheldon is unable to talk about his mother's death even when his wife asks him what he can remember.

Everyone probably has personal knowledge, feelings, and thoughts about themselves that they have avoided talking about to others. Some people may conceal painful memories of early childhood experiences such as having been sexually abused; others may conceal information about upsetting events such as failures in a close relationship or in a work setting.

Having experienced a traumatic event early in one's life can lead to enduring physical and emotional problems. Survey studies of college students and working adults conducted by James Pennebaker (1989) indicated that the experience of early childhood traumas was related to the likelihood of having health problems in adulthood and frequency of visits to a physician or a health center. Severity of health problems, however, tended to be worse for individuals who reported being sexually abused in childhood, compared to individuals who experienced either the death or divorce of parents.

In Figure 5.1 we summarize the results of survey studies on the strength of the "confiding-illness relationship" conducted by Pennebaker and his colleagues among college freshmen, upper level undergraduates, and working adults. Research participants in these studies were divided into different groups based on whether they had confided in others about the trauma. The three groups were (a) no trauma, (b) trauma and confided, and (c) trauma and not confided. Overall, not disclosing to anyone was associated with the greatest incidence of physical illness and psychological distress (see Pennebaker, Colder, & Sharp, 1988; Pennebaker & Hoover, 1985; Pennebaker & Susman, 1988). These findings were not affected by the size of an individual's social network (e.g., number of close friends). Thus, not confiding in others about a traumatic event, regardless of the nature of the trauma, accounts for differences in health among the trauma groups.

Although Pennebaker's research focused on confiding about traumatic experiences, people may avoid talking about all types of feelings, thoughts, and experiences that are considered to be embarrassing or upsetting. For instance, a person might conceal information or hide fears about being rejected in an intimate relationship, and this reserve may have negative effects on physical and psychological health.

Larson and Chastain (1990) developed a scale to measure how much individuals hide information that is perceived as threatening or negative. Items in the 10-item Self-Concealment Scale (see Table 5.1) focus on three components: (a) a tendency to keep matters to oneself (e.g., "There are lots of things about me that I keep to myself"),

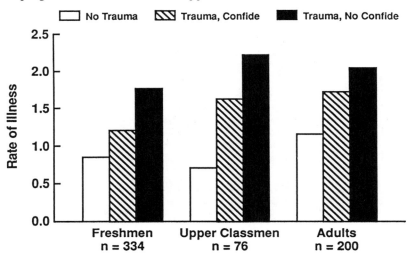

Figure 5.1. Rate of Illness Among Individuals Who Reported Experiencing No Trauma, Traumatic Experiences That Were Confided to Someone, or Traumas That Were Not Confided to Anyone

SOURCE: From "Confession, Inhibition, and Disease" by J. W. Pennebaker, 1989, in L. Berkowitz (Ed.), Advances in Experimental Social Psychology (Vol. 22, p. 214), New York: Academic Press. Used by permission of the author and Academic Press.

NOTE: For the freshman college students, the Y-axis (or ordinate) represents the actual number of visits to the university health center in the 4 months following the completion of a questionnaire about traumatic experiences. For upperclassmen, the X-axis represents the frequency of self-reported visits to a physician for a 6-month period preceding the completion of the questionnaire about traumatic experiences. For the adult sample, the Y-axis represents the number of self-reported major and minor illnesses in the year preceding filling out the questionnaire.

(b) having secret or negative thoughts about oneself that have been told to no one or only to a few others (e.g., "I have negative thoughts about myself that I never share with anyone"), and (c) fears about what would happen if the concealed information were revealed to others (e.g., "If I shared all my secrets with my friends, they'd like me less")

Adult subjects (average age 42 years) completed the Self-Concealment Scale, as well as self-report measures of physical symptoms (how often they were bothered by symptoms such as back pain, headache, and muscles soreness), anxiety, and depression. Results indicated that persons who scored highest on the Self-Concealment Scale had significantly more bodily symptoms, anxiety, and depression than did persons who scored lowest on the Self-Concealment Scale. The relationship between the tendency to conceal upsetting

Table 5.1 Self-Concealment Scale

---

1. I have an important secret that I haven't shared with anyone.
2. If I shared all my secrets with my friends, they'd like me less.
3. There are lots of things about me that I keep to myself.
4. Some of my secrets have really tormented me.
5. When something happens to me, I tend to keep it to myself.
6. I'm often afraid I'll reveal something I don't want to.
7. Telling a secret often backfires and I wish I hadn't told it.
8. I have a secret that is so private I would lie if anybody asked me about it.
9. My secrets are too embarrassing to share with others.
10. I have negative thoughts about myself that I never share with anyone.

NOTE: The scale is a 5-point Likert scale, with item responses ranging from *strongly disagree* (1) to *strongly agree* (5). The greater the score, the greater the tendency to conceal uncomfortable thoughts, feelings, and information about oneself from others.
SOURCE: From "Self-concealment: Conceptualization, Measurement, and Health Implications" by D. G. Larson and R. L. Chastain, 1990, *Journal of Social and Clinical Psychology, 9*, p. 445. Reprinted by permission of the authors and Guilford Press.

information and the incidence of physical symptoms, anxiety, and depression still occurred when measures of social support (e.g., how much support they had received from different people, number of close friends and close relatives) were controlled for statistically.

Larson and Chastain's subjects also completed the Self-Disclosure Index discussed earlier (Miller et al., 1983). The version of the scale that was used asked subjects to indicate their willingness to disclose in the future to a same-sex stranger. No significant relationship was found between this self-disclosure measure and the health indices, indicating that willingness to self-disclose (at least to strangers) was not related to health outcomes.

❧ Why Is Disclosure Beneficial and Nondisclosure Harmful?

Carol, 17, finds herself spending time each day binge-eating. She rapidly consumes lots of food in a short period of time, and then she forces herself to vomit. She does not tell anyone about her behavior because she feels ashamed about what she is doing. Not telling anyone confirms her belief that her behavior is bad.

Helen Rose, 75, was born in Poland. During World War II she spent 2 years in a concentration camp. She was the only member of her family to survive the war. After the war she moved to Canada, where she eventually married and had and raised two children. Helen Rose never talked about her experiences in the concentration camp to either her husband or her children. Recently she participated in an interview study of survivors of the Holocaust. She cried frequently during the interview, but she also felt a sense of relief that she was able to talk about feelings that had been bottled up for 50 years.

The results we have reviewed indicate that the failure to confide in others about a traumatic event affects the health of trauma victims. Also the tendency to conceal *any* information that is threatening to the self is correlated with physical and emotional problems. In this section we consider why disclosing or not disclosing is related to health outcomes.

Nondisclosure can lead to feeling ashamed and guilty. People may conceal certain information or occasionally lie because they are ashamed or embarrassed by what has happened to them. Individuals who discover that someone is concealing something may also infer that the information is "bad" or "shameful." Individuals who conceal certain facts also may conclude that the nondisclosed information represents something negative or undesirable about themselves.

According to Bem's (1972) self-perception theory, "individuals come to 'know' their own attitudes, emotions, and other internal states partially by inferring them from observation of their own overt behavior and/or circumstances in which this behavior occurs" (p. 2). The act of concealing or disclosing information about the self can influence how the information is evaluated, as well as how individuals feel about themselves.

An experiment conducted by Fishbein and Laird (1979) documents how disclosing or concealing information about one's self influences how it is evaluated. Subjects were told that an experiment involved the validation of tests that measured aspects of "social and nonsocial intelligence." They were given an ambiguous score of "4.6" that supposedly measured their performance. The research participants next were asked to discuss the experiment with another subject (actually a confederate of the experimenter). In a "conceal" condition, subjects were instructed not to reveal their score to the confederate, but in a "disclose" condition, they were asked to reveal their score. After the conversation, subjects filled out a questionnaire including an item about how satisfied they were with their performance on the alleged intelligence tests. As expected, subjects in the disclose condition, who had divulged their score to the confederate in the discussion, were more satisfied with their fictitious test score than subjects who had concealed this information.

Fishbein and Laird's results indicate why self-disclosure may be beneficial to persons who have had upsetting experiences. The act of self-disclosure may relieve feelings of guilt and shame over difficulties that were previously kept hidden. The act of disclosure may help persons see themselves more positively because they have divulged the information. On the other hand, persons who have not disclosed to anyone about painful events in their lives may feel worse and more ashamed about themselves because they infer from the act of concealing that the information is negative. For instance, a teenager who was sexually abused as a child may have concealed this information from her family. The decision to hide the information may compound the teenager's sense of guilt. She might say to herself, "I must have really done something wrong if I haven't been able to tell anyone. If I hadn't done anything wrong, then I should have been able to tell someone in the family or at least gotten help from the counselor at school."

Nondisclosure (as inhibition) increases physiological stress. The decision to conceal information about significant personal experiences requires physiological and mental work. James Pennebaker (Pennebaker, 1989; Pennebaker & Hoover, 1985) developed a theory of inhibition, arguing that the failure to disclose upsetting events requires the expenditure of energy or effort. The inhibition of one's thoughts and feelings represented by nondisclosure is stressful and is expected to harm one's physical and psychological health. Pennebaker (1989) wrote:

> 1. To actively inhibit one's thoughts, feelings, or behaviors requires physiological work. By active inhibition, we mean that individuals must consciously restrain, hold back, or in some way exert effort to *not* think, feel, or behave. . . .
> 2. In the short run, inhibition is reflected by increases in SCL [skin conductance level, which is associated with more perspiration on the

palm of the hand]. Over time, the work of inhibition serves as a cumulative stressor on the body, which increases the probability of illness and other stress-related physical and psychological problems. Active inhibition can be viewed as one of many general stressors that affect the mind and body. Obviously, the harder one must work at inhibiting, the greater stress on the body.

3. Active inhibition is also associated with potentially deleterious changes in information processing. In holding back significant thoughts and feelings associated with an event, individuals typically do not process the event fully. By not talking about an inhibited event, for example, individuals usually do not translate the event into language which . . . aids in the understanding and assimilation of the event. Consequently, significant experiences that are inhibited are likely to surface in the forms of ruminations, dreams, and associated cognitive symptoms. (p. 231)

When persons choose to avoid disclosing certain personal experiences, the short-term physiological changes associated with inhibition increase susceptibility to illness. However, if people can *confront* the information by talking with others or by thinking actively about what happened, including connecting emotions with the experiences, the negative effects of inhibition can be overcome. Pennebaker (1989) described the benefits of disclosure as confrontation in the following manner:

1. The act of confronting a trauma immediately reduces the physiological work of inhibition. During confrontation, reduction in autonomic activity such as SCL [skin conductance level] is evident. Over time, if individuals continue to confront and thereby resolve the trauma, the overall physiological work is reduced, thereby lowering the overall stress level on the body.

2. More significant, however, is that confronting a trauma helps individuals to understand and assimilate the event. By talking or writing about previously inhibited experiences, individuals translate the event into language. Once encoded linguistically, individuals can more readily understand, find meaning in, or attain closure of the experience. (p. 231)

Pennebaker viewed not talking about significant personal experiences as inhibition. In turn, inhibiting (or not disclosing) one's thoughts and feelings is predicted to place cumulative stress on the body and to increase susceptibility to illness. On the other hand, if

individuals who usually avoid disclosing about traumatic or upsetting events are permitted to "confront" or disclose about what
happened in a "safe" setting, they might be able to reduce long-term
stress and stress-related physical ailments.

An experiment conducted by Pennebaker and Beall (1986) demonstrates how having individuals disclose about traumatic events
in one's life influences long-term health. Forty-six college students
who were placed in individual rooms were randomly assigned to
write either about the most stressful and traumatic events in their
lives or about trivial topics for 15 minutes each day for 4 consecutive
days. Among subjects assigned to write about traumatic events, one
group wrote about the facts surrounding the trauma but not their
feelings about what happened; a second group wrote about their
feelings about what happened but not about the facts; and a third
group wrote about their feelings *and* the facts concerning the traumatic event.

Pennebaker and Beall (1986) collected data on blood pressure and
self-reported negative moods (e.g., feeling nervous, sad, guilty, anxious) both before and after the writing of the essays each day. The
subjects whose essays addressed either "facts and emotions combined" or "emotions only" experienced increased blood pressure and
negative moods, compared to the "only facts" or "control" subjects.
However, in the long term, subjects in the "emotions only," as well
as those in the "facts and emotions combined condition," reported
fewer health problems (e.g., ulcers, high blood pressure, colds or
flu, migraine headaches), compared to those in the "only facts" and
"control" conditions. Perhaps most important, for 6 months after writing the essays, subjects in the "facts and emotions combined condition" visited the student health center significantly less often than did
subjects in the other conditions.

More recently, Pennebaker, Kiecolt-Glaser, and Glaser (1988b) extended Pennebaker and Beall's (1986) findings. Pennebaker et al.
(1988b) found that subjects who wrote short essays about their
thoughts and feelings about a traumatic experience, over 4 consecutive days, were less likely to visit the university health center over
the next 6 weeks because of illness, compared to a control group
(who wrote about trivial topics on each of the 4 writing days). In

addition, subjects who wrote about their experiences with traumas showed improved immune system functioning 6 weeks later, compared to the control subjects. (Immunological functioning was measured by checking the white blood cell lymphocyte response to stimulation by substances foreign to the blood.) This research on disclosure and immune functioning has generated some controversy about the benefits on immune functioning of a brief experimental manipulation involving subjects disclosing past traumatic events (see Neale, Cox, Valdimarsdottir, & Stone, 1988). The evidence appears strong, however, that the positive effects on health of confronting a traumatic event (e.g., by writing about what happened) may be mediated, in part, by changes in immunological functioning (Pennebaker, Kiecolt-Glaser, & Glaser, 1988a).

Pennebaker's work suggests that if inhibitory processes are maintained over a long period of time (such as in the failure to confide to others about traumatic events that occurred in childhood), they operate as long-term stressors that increase the probability of stress-related illnesses. If people are able to confront or disclose a trauma, however, they experience an improvement in health that may be due to a short-term reduction in inhibition.

If Pennebaker is correct that inhibitory processes are associated with the failure to disclose about traumatic events, it should be possible to show that disclosing a traumatic event reduces autonomic activity involved with behavioral inhibition. Pennebaker demonstrated this finding in two studies (Pennebaker, Hughes, & O'Heeron, 1987). Individuals who talked into a tape recorder showed lower levels in skin conductance (a measure of reduced inhibitory activity) when they talked about upsetting events in their lives than about superficial topics. Also in this research, "high disclosers" (individuals who displayed more emotion in their voices, such as crying and a wavering voice), compared to "low disclosers," showed the greater decrease in skin conductance while talking about traumatic events. It appears that individuals who can "let go" while talking about a traumatic event may be expected to show positive effects by reducing the physiological work of inhibition and possibly showing improvements in immune system functioning and better long-term health.

Nondisclosure increases obsessional thinking. The experience of traumatic life events may leave vivid memories that are difficult to forget. Someone who has had an unhappy marriage may be obsessed by the failure to have had a successful relationship. An adult whose mother is deceased may have guilt feelings about the part he played in her death even though she died from natural causes. A student who failed a major exam may persist in worrying about whether she should stay in college.

If unwanted negative thoughts enter consciousness, they may cause considerable personal distress. These unwanted thoughts can create doubts about one's self-worth; raise concerns about the past, present, and future; and lower confidence about one's ability to overcome problems and to make sense of difficult life experiences.

A problem arises, however, when people try to avoid unpleasant thoughts either by not thinking about what happened or by not divulging feelings and thoughts to anyone. The more one may try to avoid talking about a traumatic life event, the more difficult it might be to get rid of the unwanted thoughts. Recall in Pennebaker and O'Heeron's (1984) study how persons who were less likely to talk with friends about their spouse's suicide or accidental death had more difficulty getting thoughts about the death out of their mind. In turn, individuals who spent more time thinking about their spouse's death had more health problems. The difficulty in talking to a friend about the spouse's death may have increased obsessive thinking about the sudden death of the spouse. The stress associated with the obsessive thinking, in turn, may have led to an increase in health problems.

Research conducted by Wegner, Schneider, Carter, and White (1987) demonstrates that people who try to suppress certain thoughts may become preoccupied later with the thoughts they seek to avoid. Subjects who were instructed to "try not to think of a white bear" would think about it more than once every minute, indicating that the suppression of the unwanted thought was not successful. Wegner et al. (1987) stated that a "paradoxical effect of thought suppression is that it produces a preoccupation with the suppressed thought" (p. 8).

An advantage of disclosing information about stressful life experiences is that obsession with certain unwanted feelings should stop (Pennebaker & O'Heeron, 1984). Persons who try hard to suppress thoughts may actually become more preoccupied with the unwanted thoughts, compared to persons who write about or confide in others about the same thoughts. Self-disclosure thus may provide a release from thinking about upsetting events, allowing the person to organize and make sense of what happened (see Horowitz, 1976; Meichenbaum, 1977; Silver, Boon, & Stones, 1983; Silver & Wortman, 1980).

Self-disclosure and social support. The psychological benefits of self-disclosure about an upsetting experience, as in the description of Pennebaker's research, could have derived from talking with a confidant, writing down thoughts and feelings on paper, or speaking about what happened into a microphone with no one present. The *social* benefits of self-disclosure, however, derive from the reactions that others provide. Briefly we summarize the types of social support that can be provided by self-disclosure in a relationship, based on a taxonomy of supportive functions suggested by Wills (1985, 1990). The socially mediated benefits of disclosing to a confidant include obtaining esteem support, informational support, instrumental support, and motivational support.

1. *Esteem support.* Upsetting life experiences can represent a threat to one's self-esteem, raising doubts about a person's worth and ability to cope. An important benefit in sharing feelings and thoughts with others may be to feel accepted, loved, and valued even though one is having difficulties. The sense of acceptance that occurs in esteem support can reduce a person's anxiety about troubling events and perhaps can strengthen personal beliefs about being in control of significant areas of life (Sarason, Sarason, & Pierce, 1990). Esteem support may occur when a disclosure target listens attentively, shares similar personal experiences, avoids criticism, or offers sympathy (Taylor, Falke, Mazel, & Hilsberg, 1988; Wills, 1985).

2. *Informational support.* Another person might be able to offer information, advice, and guidance in coping with a problem. The

success of informational support depends, in part, on the help seekers' willingness to divulge information about their upsetting situation, which, it is hoped, allows listeners to understand their needs and provide support. For instance, cancer patients may talk about their problems in a cancer-related support group to gain information about medical issues and strategies for coping with the illness (Taylor et al., 1988). College students who are doing poorly in their course work may describe school-related problems to an academic advisor, hoping for advice on how to improve study skills.

Informational support may operate directly in the sense of someone providing advice or mapping out a course of action. Informational support sometimes may operate indirectly by allowing individuals to assess their abilities and capacities via comparison with the abilities and capacities of other people (Festinger, 1954; Wills, 1985). Persons can judge how well they are coping with an illness, for instance, by seeing how others who are similar to them are handling the same problem. Persons not only may desire information to evaluate how well they are coping but also may be motivated by the need for the evaluation to turn out favorably for themselves, where the search for information is influenced by a self-enhancement motive (Wills, 1981). Persons under stress may want to know that they are coping better than others, that they are not as unfortunate as some others, or that their problems are not due to personal deficiencies.

3. *Instrumental support.* Other people can provide instrumental support, such as helping with food shopping or child care for someone who has been physically injured or is ill. If persons who need assistance cannot or will not tell others that something is seriously wrong, instrumental support (the most tangible form of assistance) will not be available.

4. *Motivational support.* Even if problems are not easily resolvable, other people can offer encouragement, or motivational support. For instance, if a person is in an unsatisfactory job situation, it might be difficult to find a new job quickly or to change the working conditions. If we can share with others what has happened, they might be able to reassure us that matters will improve, that efforts to look for a new job will be successful, and that "we can get

through the worst." On the one hand, motivational support may encourage individuals to persist in coping with upsetting situations in which the ordinary tendency might be to give up and become depressed. On the other hand, if motivational comments by a confidant sound contrived or too cheerful, they might be seen as unhelpful rather than helpful by the distressed person (Coyne, Wortman, & Lehman, 1988).

❧ When Self-Disclosure Is Not Beneficial

Bill, 20, and Mark, 21, are juniors at a state university. They are flying together to Florida for spring break. Bill is uncomfortable about flying, and he tells Mark about being nervous. Mark, in turn, describes an unpleasant experience when, on another flight, his plane had mechanical problems. As the plane takes off, neither of them is feeling very good. Somehow, talking about their fears made them feel worse rather than better.

Alice, 41, lost one of her two children, a daughter, in a car accident 3 years ago. Alice recently told a friend at work that she continued to grieve over the loss of her daughter. The friend said in reply, "You should try to get over her death. Your daughter had a full life, and you still have another child who is healthy." Alice felt that her friend's comments were not helpful; she did not talk again at work about her daughter's death.

We have emphasized in this chapter how talking and/or writing about upsetting life events can have positive psychological and physical effects in coping with stress. However, it is useful to consider the conditions under which self-disclosure may not be helpful. In this section we examine how self-disclosure itself may intensify unpleasant feelings and how others' nonsupportive reactions to the self-disclosure of upsetting events can worsen negative feelings.

Self-disclosure under conditions of heightened self-awareness. Self-disclosure may be useful in coping with stress because it allows insight and understanding about one's difficulties. However, according to Duval and Wicklund's (1972) theory of objective self-awareness, heightened self-awareness occurs when someone discloses or anticipates talking about intimate information. If the information is negative, it may focus attention on real or imagined weaknesses and faults, contributing to an individual's feeling worse about him- or herself. The self-awareness associated with high self-disclosure thus may aggravate one's negative mood state by focusing on the discrepancy between the real self and an ideal self.

An experiment conducted by Archer, Hormuth, and Berg (1982) illustrates how the disclosure of intimate information under conditions of self-awareness can be unpleasant. Subjects were assigned to talk about either high intimacy topics or low intimacy topics. The high intimacy topics encouraged subjects to make negative statements about the self (e.g., "Whether or not I need other people to be happy," "My ups and downs in mood"), whereas the low intimacy topics encouraged them to make positive statements about the self (e.g., "The type of job I would like to have," "My favorite ways of spending free time"). To intensify subjects' self-awareness, half of the subjects talked into a microphone about their assigned topics in a cubicle in front of a large mirror, while the other half of the subjects talked into a microphone about their assigned topics in a cubicle with no mirror present. The combination of being assigned to talk about intimate topics in the presence of a large mirror was expected to focus attention on one's feelings and to intensify negative feelings associated with the disclosure of intimate content.

The results indicated that subjects who were in the "mirror-high intimacy" condition reported the least enjoyment of the self-description task. There was also a trend for independent judges to rate the subjects in this condition as being the most nervous. Subjects in the mirror-high intimacy condition took the longest to begin talking on each of their assigned topics, and these subjects were rated by independent judges as having provided the least complete self-descriptions. Thus the results supported the conclusion that intimate self-disclosure may intensify negative feelings under certain conditions (e.g., in the presence of a large mirror or an audience) by bringing one's problems and difficulties into focus.

Self-disclosure that focuses on personal problems may heighten negative affect immediately, but it is likely to have positive, long-term effects. For instance, in the study by Pennebaker and Beall (1986) described earlier, it was found that writing about both the feelings and facts associated with a traumatic event (trauma combination condition) caused relatively high blood pressure and negative feelings about the self following completion of the essays. However, these subjects, after 6 months, were healthier physically (based on fewest visits to a health center), compared to subjects who wrote essays about trivial topics, only facts associated with the traumatic event, or only feelings associated with the traumatic event.

Talking about negative feelings in anticipation of an upsetting event. The timing of self-disclosure (either before or after an upsetting event has occurred) may influence coping reactions. If persons anticipate going through a stressful event, disclosure of feelings *before* the stressful event is experienced may magnify negative affect. But persons who talk about their feelings *after* the stressful event may undergo a positive experience represented by ventilating negative feelings or gaining insight about what happened (Derlega, Margulis, & Winstead, 1987; Freud, 1904/1954; Pennebaker, 1989). The impact of timing of self-disclosure has not been considered in past studies in coping with stress. However, studies conducted by Hobfoll and London (1986) and Costanza, Derlega, and Winstead (1988) suggest a situation in which self-disclosure in anticipation of a stressful event may not be beneficial.

Hobfoll and London (1986) studied coping reactions of Israeli women whose boyfriends, husbands, or relatives had been mobilized into the Israeli military during the 1982 Israel-Lebanon conflict. The women reported greater psychological distress (state anxiety and state depression during the current week) if they had friends or neighbors with whom to talk. Scores on an intimacy with friends scale (e.g., "I have friends with whom I can speak freely about what is important to me," "I have friends that seem to bring out the best qualities in me") were positively correlated with anxiety. In addition, amount of social support received during the crisis period (e.g., sharing feelings, tangible assistance, or advice received) was positively correlated with depression.

Hobfoll and London (1986) suggested that interacting frequently with friends and neighbors who were also undergoing the same uncertainty (e.g., having a male relative or friend in combat) may have produced a "pressure cooker" effect. Talking with other members

of one's social support group who were undergoing the same unpleasant experiences may have helped spread rumors and led to
exaggerated accounts of what actually was happening in the war,
which, in turn, may have increased psychological distress. In addition, for women with high coping traits (based on relatively high
self-esteem and sense of mastery scores), intimacy with friends and
the amount of social support received were positively correlated
with amount of emotional strain. For women with low coping traits,
no relationship was found between intimacy with friends and/or
social support and negative emotional state. Women with high coping
traits may have more close relationships. By disclosing and being
recipients of the intimate disclosures of others who are undergoing
a stressful event, "high copers" may be susceptible to greater emotional strains than "low copers" who have fewer intimate friends
(Hobfoll & London, 1986; Kessler, McLeod, & Wetherington, 1985).

An experiment by Costanza et al. (1988) also indicates that the disclosure of feelings associated with an impending stressful event
may be associated with a relatively high level of negative affect.
Subjects who signed up for a study with a same-sex friend were told
that the research involved "participant modeling" and that they
would be asked to guide a tarantula through a maze after watching
a model (the experimenter) do it. Subjects were assigned to one of
three "talk" conditions on the basis of how they spent their time
before they actually handled the spider: talking with a friend about
their feelings concerning the task with the spider, problem-solving
about how they expected to handle the participant modeling task,
or discussing topics unrelated to the task with the tarantula.

Negative mood states, based on anxiety and depression scores,
were higher in the disclosure-of-feelings condition than in the problem-solving and irrelevant-talk conditions. A behavioral measure of
fear of the spider also was obtained on the basis of how near the
subjects were willing to pull the spider (enclosed in a cart with sides
made out of a clear fishing line netting) toward themselves. Subjects
were less willing to allow the spider to be pulled as close as possible
in the disclosure-of-feelings (35%) than in the problem-solving (64%)
and unrelated-talk (71%) conditions. These results indicate that talking
about one's feelings with a friend in anticipation of a stressful event
is less beneficial than talking with a friend about problem-solving

or unrelated content. In addition, some subjects also were assessed in an "alone" condition, where they waited by themselves in anticipation of handling the tarantula. These "alone" subjects, similar to the subjects in the disclosure-of-feelings condition, had relatively high anxiety and behavioral fear scores in comparison to subjects in the problem-solving and unrelated-talk conditions.

In Costanza et al.'s (1988) study, both friends expected to undergo the stressful event (going through the participant modeling task involving the tarantula). We can speculate that disclosing one's feelings to a friend magnifies negative affect when both friends expect to undergo the unpleasant experience, but not when only one of them expects to go through it. Depending on the circumstances, interacting with people whom we know may mean talking with someone equally stressed or with someone relatively unaffected. The psychological state of the other surely influences his or her effectiveness, and this influence may be especially the case when feelings are being shared. Interacting with a friend who shares the same concerns may accentuate both persons' feelings. In other situations, such as when someone's spouse or child dies, only the bereaved person has experienced a direct, personal loss. Disclosure of feelings to a friend experiencing much less grief may be effective in reducing negative affect because friends can serve as concerned listeners without feeling pressure to ventilate their own feelings. Consistent with this view, Derlega, Abdo, Winstead, and Swinth (1990) found that disclosure of feelings with a friend who was not expecting to undergo the same stressful event did not generate more negative affect, compared to problem-solving and unrelated-talk conditions, whereas disclosure of feelings to a friend who also expected to undergo the stressful event generated more negative affect than in the other conversation topic conditions.

We have suggested how disclosure of feelings associated with a future stressor may not be beneficial. It would be inappropriate, however, to conclude that no benefits are derived from talking with a confidant or joining a support group in anticipation of a stressful event. In fact, confidants or co-participants in a support group may promote coping by increasing people's confidence in their ability to cope with a stressful event, by providing useful information, and by making one another feel accepted (Sarason et al., 1990). The danger of focusing exclusively on disclosure of feelings as a coping strategy in anticipation of a stressful event is to make the impending event (which may seem ambiguous and uncertain) appear more threatening than it originally did.

Recipients of intimate self-disclosure who provide "negative" social support. People who have had upsetting experiences may talk with friends and family to obtain social support. Others' supportive reactions may satisfy specific needs that arise during a crisis (such as conveying the impression that the distressed person is accepted, cared for, and understood), as well as providing information and tangible assistance. However, the feedback that others provide is not inevitably supportive. For instance, people who have experienced a death in the family report that how others responded to them during the bereavement was frequently unhelpful (Davidowitz & Myrick, 1984). Cancer patients may notice that they are treated differently once others learn that they have cancer, a change that leads the patients to feel alienated and estranged from friends and family (Peters-Golden, 1982; Wortman & Conway, 1985).

Lehman, Ellard, and Wortman (1986) conducted a study of 94 people who had lost either a spouse or a child in a motor vehicle accident 4 to 6 years earlier. The bereaved persons were asked to describe support attempts from others that were helpful and unhelpful. The support attempts that were most frequently mentioned as helpful included contact with similar others, the opportunity to express, expressions of concern, and the mere presence of another person. Unhelpful support attempts that were most frequently mentioned included giving advice, encouraging recovery, forced cheerfulness, and identification with feelings (e.g., "I know what you feel"). Interestingly, control respondents (who had not lost either a spouse or a child in a motor vehicle accident) were asked what they would do if they were trying to provide support to someone who had lost either a child or a spouse. These control respondents rarely mentioned that they would use such unhelpful support tactics as giving advice, minimizing the loss, or encouraging recovery. Instead they said that they would be available for the victim, indicate concern, and provide opportunities for a discussion of feelings (which were the tactics that the bereaved saw as helpful).

The control respondents were aware of what support behaviors would be appropriate to aid a bereaved person. However, on the basis of the bereaved respondents' descriptions in Lehman et al.'s (1986) study, other people often say and do things that are not helpful. Potential supporters may experience considerable anxiety and tension when they hear another person describe a life crisis. Potential support providers may become upset themselves, thus making it difficult to provide effective support, reducing them to offering platitudes such as "I know how you feel" or "things will get better" (Lehman et al., 1986, p. 443). In other words, we may know the right thing to say; we just do not always say it.

A study by Ashworth, Furman, Chaikin, and Derlega (1976) illustrates how self-disclosure input that focuses on personal problems can generate discomfort and stress in a listener. As part of a supposed study on perception, male subjects heard a male confederate begin to disclose information for about 2 minutes. In the high intimacy condition, the confederate revealed personal information concerning difficulties in an opposite-sex relationship. In the low intimacy condition, he revealed superficial information about one of his classes at the university. The confederate and the subjects did not know one another at the beginning of the session. Physiological (skin conductance and heart rate) and self-report (subjects' comfort during the experiment) measures were obtained.

Subjects showed a greater increase in skin conductance level and heart rate in high than in low disclosure intimacy conditions. In addition, subjects felt less comfortable in high than in low intimacy conditions, and they reported that the confederate influenced their comfort ratings more in the high than in the low intimacy condition. A trend was also found for withdrawal in the high intimacy condition: Subjects were less likely to respond verbally after the confederate's disclosure input in the high (25%) than in the low intimacy condition (50%).

Ashworth et al.'s (1976) results indicate how intimate disclosure about personal problems may create discomfort in a listener. In this study the intimate disclosure input was provided by a stranger, a variable that might be considered as inappropriate, unusual, and presumably stressful. However, although friends and family members are closely acquainted, they too might undergo stress in discussing intimate content because they may feel more responsibility about alleviating a loved one's problems (Lehman et al., 1986).

❧ How Many Confidants Are Enough?

> Rajiv, 48, is a professor at a business college. He had been on leave
> for one semester to obtain treatment for cancer. When he returned to
> teach, a number of friends individually came by his office to wish him
> well and to ask about his health. Some of them even talked about their
> own health problems. Although Rajiv was pleased with their interest
> in him, he felt tired of talking about his illness over and over again.

Survey research indicates that individuals who are able to talk to someone about upsetting life events are generally healthier than those who do not have a confidant (Brown, Bhrolchain, & Harris, 1975; Lowenthal & Haven, 1968; Miller & Lefcourt, 1983). A question arises, however, about how many confidants are enough.

The perception of being cared for, loved, and valued is a major ingredient in social support (Reis, 1990; Sarason et al., 1990). Having one major confidant, such as a spouse, family member, or close friend to talk with, presumably should be sufficient in many instances to gain this benefit. However, insofar as individuals cope with various life events, it is probably unrealistic to expect that one confidant can satisfy all of one's needs for social support. The physically ill, for instance, have needs for various kinds of support. A cancer patient may want to discuss the illness with her husband in order to know he cares about her, but she also may discuss her difficulties with members of a cancer support group to share concerns with others who have similar experiences, to receive advice, or to learn skills in coping with the illness (Taylor et al., 1988).

A survey study conducted by Stokes (1983) found a curvilinear relationship between the number of confidants and satisfaction with social support. Satisfaction with one's social network increased up to having seven confidants, but increases in the number of confidants beyond this point were not related to increased satisfaction. Having more than one confidant has a number of advantages: If one confidant is not available, another might be substituted, or different confidants might be expert at providing different kinds of support (we may value the emotional support of a friend who indicates concern for us, but relatives might be more useful in providing financial assistance in a crisis). However, if the number of confidants (or close social relationships) becomes too large, the costs of developing and maintaining the relationships (e.g., obligation to provide support for the other person) may outweigh the potential advantages (Stokes, 1983). For instance, as noted earlier, in Hobfoll and London's (1986) study, Israeli women who had a male friend or relative in combat suffered greater stress if they had many friends who faced the same upsetting situation.

ϫ Conclusions

Sidney Jourard (1971b), a clinical psychologist and pioneer in research on self-disclosure, wrote: "The time is not far off when it will be possible to demonstrate with adequately controlled experiments the nature and degree of correlations between levels and amounts of self-disclosure and proneness to illness and/or an early death age" (p. 36). This chapter demonstrates the health benefits for individuals who can disclose their deepest feelings associated with traumatic and upsetting events. Particularly in the review of Pennebaker's studies of individuals who have undergone traumas, those who can disclose about painful experiences may be able to reduce the psychological stress associated with inhibiting certain thoughts and feelings.

Self-disclosure is a vehicle for obtaining social support that might not be available if other people did not know about one's difficulties. Socially mediated benefits associated with disclosing to a confidant include esteem support, information support, instrumental support, and motivational support.

Despite the benefits of self-disclosure, individuals incur risks in sharing upsetting personal experiences with others. The disclosure of negative feelings may at least temporarily generate discomfort in the speaker and cause the listener to feel upset and embarrassed. Another risk is that if negative feelings are aroused in the listener, the discloser may experience rejection. Overall, though, the advantages of self-disclosure are apparent. Self-disclosure about personal events that are perceived as stressful can improve health, as well as increase one's self-esteem and ability to cope.

6

Epilogue

Connie, 22, has dated Ken, 24, for 5 months. They have enjoyed dating one another, and they even talk occasionally about getting engaged. Connie is troubled, however, about Ken's tendency to shrug off talking about some things that are bothering him. For instance, Ken has had trouble finding a steady job since he graduated from college. Connie thinks that Ken is upset about this problem, but he refuses to talk about it with her. Connie wants Ken to know that he can count on her support if he needs help. But she worries about their relationship if they can't talk about things that are important to them.

As the opening anecdote for the chapter indicates, and as we have seen throughout the book, decisions about self-disclosure can affect our relationships with others. Self-disclosure determines how much others know about us, but it also may influence others' impressions about what we think and feel about them. In concluding the book, we would like you to fill out the true-false test below to review what you have learned about self-disclosure in close relationships. You also might administer the quiz to someone who has not read the book to see how well popular beliefs about self-disclosure agree with the results of research. Then we will present some final thoughts.

❧ Self-Disclosure Quiz (True or False)

1. The level of self-disclosure in a conversation defines the level of intimacy or closeness of the partners' relationship.

2. The major function or goal of self-disclosure is to ventilate one's feelings after undergoing a stressful event.

3. How much someone discloses is exclusively determined by how much the discloser is willing to say.

4. The content of self-disclosure is limited to evaluative self-disclosures (that is, the disclosure of personal feelings, judgments, and opinions).

5. If someone discloses personal information about themselves, that will inevitably lead to the development of a close relationship between the discloser and the disclosure recipient.

6. As people develop a close relationship, the only pattern of self-disclosure is for individuals to disclose gradually about themselves over time.

7. The notion of subcultural differences between women and men may be useful in understanding gender-linked differences in self-disclosure.

8. In a privacy regulation model of self-disclosure, privacy represents control over the amount and kind of information exchange that persons have with one another.

9. Early childhood experiences in interacting with parents probably have no effects on one's willingness as an adult to self-disclose to a relationship partner.

10. Partners in dating relationships are unlikely to perceive certain topics as "off-limits" to talk about with their partner.

11. When a parent and a child keep a "secret" that is hidden from the other parent, there are no side effects for the family.

12. For people who have had a traumatic event in their lives, confiding in others about the trauma can be a healthy response.

The answers to the test are as follows:

1. *False.* Level of self-disclosure is not synonymous with the intimacy or closeness of a relationship. Self-disclosure contributes to the development of a close relationship (e.g., to make inferences about how well the partners get along or like one another, to help one another in solving relationship problems). However, people may feel close to one another without necessarily exchanging intimate disclosures (e.g., partners who fall in love at first sight,

share many activities together, or are able to resolve differences of opinion without conflict).

2. *False.* Although a major function of self-disclosure may be to ventilate feelings about a stressful event (achieve "catharsis"), there are many goals or functions of self-disclosure. Through self-disclosure we may signal to someone that we want him or her to know us better, we may wish to be validated or supported by our friends and loved ones when faced with personal difficulties, or we may seek to present a favorable impression to influence someone's judgment about us.

3. *False.* Decisions about self-disclosure are not made exclusively by the discloser. There is a negotiation by partners in close relationships (in the roles of discloser and disclosure recipient) about what they will talk about with one another. In addition, when decisions are made about self-disclosure, there are consequences not only for the individuals themselves—based on what is said— but also for the relationship itself. Hence partners may avoid talking about certain topics (e.g., a dating partner may be simultaneously involved in a sexual relationship with someone else) because they are both unable to cope at present with the implications of revealing this importation for their own relationship.

4. *False.* Although evaluative self-disclosure (especially the expression of personal feelings such as "I feel anxious") is an important class of self-disclosure, other types of self-disclosure include descriptive self-disclosures (information and facts about the self, such as "I spent a week in Florida during spring break" or "I just flunked the quiz"), as well as relational self-disclosures (disclosures about one's thoughts and feelings about a relationship or about interactions with another person). Relational self-disclosures are an important ingredient in how well couples maintain their relationships and cope with relationship conflicts.

5. *False.* Self-disclosure may signal to the disclosure recipient that the discloser is interested in developing a closer relationship. However, a disclosure recipient will react to what is said on the basis of a variety of factors, including the message itself, how long the partners have known one another, as well as the character and intentions of the discloser. It is useful to think about the relationship between self-disclosure and a close relationship unfolding

interactively through the process of mutual transformation. This statement means that there is a continuous interaction between self-disclosure and the relationship such that self-disclosure may affect the definition and direction of a relationship, and a variety of factors or transformation agents (such as relational definition, liking, relationship goals, attributions given for the discloser's behavior, liking) can affect the meaning and impact of self-disclosure.

6. *False.* Social penetration theory popularized the idea that people disclose gradually more and more about themselves as a relationship develops. However, different patterns of self-disclosure may occur in a developing relationship. Other patterns of self-disclosure in a developing relationship include a linear progression at first but shifting to a sharp decline after an initial period of openness, a pattern of increasing disclosure that eventually levels off and even declines somewhat, and the "clicking" trajectory, in which the disclosure almost immediately is highly personal.

7. *True.* From early childhood, boys and girls tend to play and socialize with same-sex peers where they may be rewarded and praised for different behaviors. On the one hand, if boys are rewarded for being self-assured, rational, and not losing control, they may underestimate the value of disclosing feelings. On the other hand, if girls are rewarded for being nurturant, affectionate, and understanding of others' needs, they may value the disclosure of feelings. Particularly when stress and conflict are experienced in a personal relationship, men and women may rely on gender stereotyped modes of communication that might lead to misunderstandings and dissatisfaction with the relationship.

8. *True.* The disclosure of personal information and feelings may create risks. Disclosure recipients may divulge this information to people who ought not to have access to the information, or the other person may get upset if a certain topic is brought up. By regulating metaphorical "boundaries" (e.g., making sure that no one else will find out what is said, deciding how to package the content of the disclosure message) the discloser, it is hoped, reduces the vulnerability associated with self-disclosure.

9. *False.* "Avoidant" persons who are uncomfortable being close to others are more inhibited in their self-disclosure, compared to "secure" and "anxious/avoidant" persons. Avoidant individuals may have had parents who were insensitive to the child's needs, leading to the development of a model of relationships based on a lack of trust and a fear of closeness.

10. *False.* We mentioned the notion of an "ethic of openness," which seems to encourage a high level of disclosure by many dating couples. However, individuals may perceive that certain topics are taboo or off-limits to talk about in an opposite-sex relationship (e.g., the stage of the relationship, one's own and the partner's other relationships).

11. *False.* Tensions may occur in families when disclosures by a parent to a child or by a child to a parent are kept secret and attempts are made to conceal the information or mislead other family members.

12. *True.* To hold back or actively avoid the disclosure of information associated with a traumatic event involves physiological and psychological work. The inhibition of one's thoughts and feelings about a traumatic event creates stress on the body and makes it difficult for the person to assimilate what happened. Confronting a trauma by means of self-disclosure may lower the overall stress level of the body and may help persons understand the traumatic event.

≈ Conclusions

A great deal still needs to be studied about self-disclosure in relationships, including understanding how relationship partners negotiate when, how, and what to talk about. What are the rules and norms governing self-disclosure between relationship partners (e.g., if taboo topics exist between partners, what are the circumstances when this information should be divulged)? Are the benefits of self-disclosure about traumatic events uniquely linked to talking with a confidant, or is it enough to, for example, talk into a microphone with no one else present? What is the impact of self-disclosure to a therapist or to a priest in confession?

This book and (we hope) your success on the quiz indicate that we have learned a great deal about the impact of self-disclosure on relationships. Particularly in the discussion of major themes presented in Chapters 2, 3, 4, and 5, we know that (a) close relationships and self-disclosure are mutually transformative, (b) subcultural differences affect self-disclosure between men and women, (c) people regulate privacy in their decisions about self-disclosure, and (d) self-disclosure may be useful in coping with stress and gaining social support ("stress-reducing disclosure"). Thus we have a better grasp of the role played by self-disclosure in relationships and more generally a better understanding of how close relationships operate.

A final thought: Think for a moment of the many similarities that humans share with other animals. Many species, like ours, build homes, care for young, compete for resources, and have relationships. Many animals, like us, are also capable of communicating—telling one another when they are in pain, frightened, or content with a meal. However, humans are probably unique in being able to reflect and put into perspective their own thoughts and feelings and then to decide whether to divulge this information to someone else. As researchers we are cautious in weighing the pros and cons of self-disclosure. Nevertheless, although disclosure involves possible risks of rejection, misunderstanding, embarrassment, and betrayal, it offers the opportunity to get to know another person and to be known by another person. Although self-disclosure by itself is not a sufficient condition for intimacy or closeness in a relationship, it provides a context for these qualities and, hence, is important in understanding a unique feature of human interaction.

References

Ainsworth, M. D. S., Blehar, M. C., Waters, E., & Wall, S. (1978). *Patterns of attachment: A psychological study of the strange situation*. Hillsdale, NJ: Lawrence Erlbaum.

Alberts, J. (1988). An analysis of couples' conversational complaints. *Communication Monographs, 55*, 184-197.

Altman, I. (1973). Reciprocity of interpersonal exchange. *Journal for the Theory of Social Behavior, 3*, 249-261.

Altman, I. (1975). *The environment and social behavior*. Belmont, CA: Brooks/Cole.

Altman, I., & Taylor, D. A. (1973). *Social penetration: The development of interpersonal relationships*. New York: Holt, Rinehart & Winston.

Altman, I., Vinsel, A., & Brown, B. H. (1981). Dialectic conceptions in social psychology: An application to social penetration and privacy regulation. In L. Berkowitz (Ed.), *Advances in experimental social psychology* (Vol. 14, pp. 107-160). New York: Academic Press.

Archer, R. L. (1987). Commentary: Self-disclosure, a very useful behavior. In V. J. Derlega & J. H. Berg (Eds.), *Self-disclosure: Theory, research, and therapy* (pp. 329-342). New York: Plenum.

Archer, R. L., & Burleson, J. A. (1980). The effects of timing and responsibility of self-disclosure on attraction. *Journal of Personality, 38,* 120-130.

Archer, R. L., Hormuth, S. E., & Berg, J. H. (1982). Avoidance of self-disclosure: An experiment under conditions of self-awareness. *Personality and Social Psychology Bulletin, 8,* 122-128.

Argyle, M., & Dean, J. (1965). Eye-contact, distance and affiliation. *Sociometry, 28,* 289-304.

Aries, E. J., & Johnson, F. L. (1983). Close friendship in adulthood: Conversational content between same-sex friends. *Sex Roles, 9,* 1183-1196.

Ashworth, C., Furman, G., Chaikin, A. L., & Derlega, V. J. (1976). Physiological responses to self-disclosure. *Journal of Humanistic Psychology, 16,* 71-80.

Baile, S. (1984, February). *A quantitative study of the consequences of self-disclosure.* Paper presented at the Annual Meeting of the Western Speech Communication Association, Albuquerque, NM.

Bavelas, J. B. (1983). Situations that lead to disqualification. *Human Communication Research, 9,* 130-145.

Baxter, L. A. (1979). Self-disclosure as a disengagement strategy. *Human Communication Research, 5,* 215-222.

Baxter, L. A. (1983). Relationship disengagement: An examination of the reversal hypothesis. *Western Journal of Speech Communication, 47,* 85-98.

Baxter, L. A. (1987). Self-disclosure and relationship disengagement. In V. J. Derlega & J. H. Berg (Eds.), *Self-disclosure: Theory, research, and therapy* (pp. 155-174). New York: Plenum.

Baxter, L. A. (1990). Dialectical contradictions in relationship development. *Journal of Social and Personal Relationships, 7,* 69-88.

Baxter, L. A. (1991, May). *Thinking dialogically about personal relationships.* Paper presented at the Conference of the International Network on Personal Relationships, Normal, IL.

Baxter, L. A., & Wilmot, W. W. (1984). "Secret tests": Social strategies for acquiring information about the state of the relationship. *Human Communication Research, 11,* 171-201.

Baxter, L. A., & Wilmot, W. W. (1985). Taboo topics in close relationships. *Journal of Social and Personal Relationships, 2,* 253-269.

Bem, D. (1972). Self-perception theory. In L. Berkowitz (Ed.), *Advances in experimental social psychology* (Vol. 6, pp. 1-62). New York: Academic Press.

Berg, J. H. (1984). The development of friendships between roommates. *Journal of Personality and Social Psychology, 46,* 346-356.

Berg, J. H. (1987). Responsiveness and self-disclosure. In V. J. Derlega & J. H. Berg (Eds.), *Self-disclosure: Theory, research, and therapy* (pp. 101-130). New York: Plenum.

Berg, J. H., & Archer, R. L. (1980). Disclosure or concern: A second look at liking for the norm-breaker. *Journal of Personality, 48,* 245-257.

Berg, J. H., & Archer, R. L. (1983). The disclosure-liking relationship: Effects of self-perception, order of disclosure, and topical similarity. *Human Communication Research, 10,* 269- 281.

Berg, J. H., & Clark, M. S. (1986). Differences in social exchange between intimate and other relationships: Gradually evolving or quickly apparent? In V. J. Derlega & B. A. Winstead (Eds.), *Friendship and social interaction* (pp. 101-128). New York: Springer Verlag.

Berg, J. H., & McQuinn, R. D. (1986). Attraction and exchange in continuing and noncontinuing dating relationships. *Journal of Personality and Social Psychology, 50,* 942-952.

Berger, C. R. (1987). Communicating under uncertainty. In M. E. Roloff & G. R. Miller (Eds.), *Interpersonal processes: New directions in communication research* (pp. 39-62). Newbury Park, CA: Sage.

Berger, C. R., & Bradac, J. J. (1982). *Language and social knowledge: Uncertainty in interpersonal relations.* London: Edward Arnold.

Bochner, A. P. (1982). On the efficacy of openness in closed relationships. In M. Burgoon (Ed.), *Communication yearbook 5* (pp. 109-124). New Brunswick, NJ: Transaction Books.

Bok, S. (1984). *Secrets: On the ethics of concealment and revelation.* New York: Vintage.

Bowlby, J. (1969). *Attachment and loss: Vol. 1. Attachment.* London: Hogarth.

Bradbury, T. N., & Fincham, F. D. (1989). Behavior and satisfaction in marriage: Prospective mediating processes. In C. Hendrick (Ed.), *Close relationships* (pp. 119-143). Newbury Park, CA: Sage.

Braithwaite, D. O. (1991). "Just how much did that wheelchair cost?": Management of privacy boundaries by persons with disabilities. *Western Journal of Speech Communication, 55,* 254-274.

Brown, G. W., Bhrolchain, M., & Harris, T. (1975). Social class and psychiatric disturbance among women in an urban population. *Sociology, 9,* 225-253.

Burgoon, J. K., Parrott, R., Le Poire, B. A., Kelley, D. L., Walther, J. B., & Perry, D. (1989). Maintaining and restoring privacy through communication in different types of relationships. *Journal of Social and Personal Relationships, 6,* 131-158.

Caldwell, M. A., & Peplau, L. A. (1982). Sex differences in same-sex friendship. *Sex Roles, 8,* 721-732.

Chaikin, A. L., & Derlega, V. J. (1974). Liking for the norm-breaker in self-disclosure. *Journal of Personality, 42,* 117-129.

Chelune, G. J. (1976). Reactions to male and female disclosure at two levels. *Journal of Personality and Social Psychology, 34,* 1000-1003.

Chelune, G. J., Robinson, J. T., & Kommor, M. J. (1984). A cognitive interactional model of intimate relationships. In V. J. Derlega (Ed.), *Communication, intimacy, and close relationships* (pp. 11-40). Orlando, FL: Academic Press.

Chelune, G. J., Skiffington, S., & Williams, C. (1981). Multidimensional analysis of observers' perceptions of self-disclosing behavior. *Journal of Personality and Social Psychology, 41*, 599-606.

Chelune, G. J., Waring, E. M., Vosk, B. N., Sultan, F. E., & Ogden, J. K. (1984). Self-disclosure and its relationship to marital intimacy. *Journal of Clinical Psychology, 40*, 216-219.

Chesler, M. A., & Barbarin, O. A. (1984). Difficulties of providing help in a crisis: Relationships between parents of children with cancer and their friends. *Journal of Social Issues, 40*(4), 113-134.

Collins, N. L., & Miller, L. C. (1991). *The disclosure-liking link: From meta-analysis towards a dynamic reconceptualization.* Unpublished manuscript, University of Southern California, Los Angeles.

Coopersmith, E. I. (1985). Teaching trainees to think in triads. *Journal of Marital and Family Therapy, 11*, 61-66.

Costanza, R. S., Derlega, V. J., & Winstead, B. A. (1988). Positive and negative forms of social support: Effects of conversational topics on coping with stress among same-sex friends. *Journal of Experimental Social Psychology, 24*, 182-193.

Coupland, J., Coupland, H., Giles, H., & Wieman, J. (1988). My life in your hands: Processes of self-disclosure in intergenerational talk. In N. Coupland (Ed.), *Styles of discourse* (pp. 201-253). London: Croom Helm.

Coyne, J. C., Wortman, C. B., & Lehman, D. R. (1988). The other side of support: Emotional over involvement and miscarried helping. In B. H. Gottlieb (Ed.), *Marshaling social support: Formats, processes, and effects* (pp. 305-330). Newbury Park, CA: Sage.

Davidowitz, M., & Myrick, R. D. (1984). Responding to the bereaved: An analysis of "helping" statements. *Research Record, 1*, 35-42.

Davis, J. D. (1978). When boy meets girl: Sex roles and the negotiation of intimacy in an acquaintance exercise. *Journal of Personality and Social Psychology, 36*, 684-692.

Deaux, K., & Major, B. (1987). Putting gender into context: An interactive model of gender-related behavior. *Psychological Review, 94*, 369-389.

Derlega, V. J., Abdo, D., Winstead, B. A., & Swinth, H. (1990). *Effects of topic of conversation and similarity of experience on coping with stress.* Unpublished manuscript, Old Dominion University, Norfolk, VA.

Derlega, V. J., & Chaikin, A. L. (1976). Norms affecting self-disclosure in men and women. *Journal of Consulting and Clinical Psychology, 44*, 376-380.

Derlega, V. J., & Chaikin, A. L. (1977). Privacy and self-disclosure in social relationships. *Journal of Social Issues, 33*(3), 102-115.

Derlega, V. J., & Grzelak, J. (1979). Appropriateness of self-disclosure. In G. J. Chelune (Ed.), *Self-disclosure: Origins, patterns, and implications of openness in interpersonal relationships* (pp. 151-176). San Francisco: Jossey-Bass.

Derlega, V. J., & Margulis, S. T. (1982). Why loneliness occurs: The interrelationship of social psychological and privacy concepts. In L. A. Peplau

& D. Perlman (Eds.), *Loneliness: A sourcebook of current theory, research and therapy* (pp. 152-165). New York: Wiley-Interscience.

Derlega, V. J., Margulis, S. T., & Winstead, B. A. (1987). A social-psychological analysis of self-disclosure in psychotherapy. *Journal of Social and Clinical Psychology, 5,* 205-215.

Derlega, V. J., Wilson, J., & Chaikin, A. L. (1976). Friendship and disclosure reciprocity. *Journal of Personality and Social Psychology, 34,* 578-582.

Derlega, V. J., Winstead, B. A., Wong, P. T. P., & Greenspan, M. (1987). Self-disclosure and relationship development: An attributional analysis. In M. E. Roloff & G. R. Miller (Eds.), *Interpersonal processes: New directions in communication research* (pp. 172-187). Newbury Park, CA: Sage.

Derlega, V. J., Winstead, B. A., Wong, P. T. P., & Hunter, S. (1985). Gender effects in an initial encounter: A case where men exceed women in disclosure. *Journal of Social and Personal Relationships, 2,* 25-44.

Dindia, K., & Allen, M. (in press). Sex differences in self-disclosure: A meta-analysis. *Psychological Bulletin.*

Duck, S. W. (1982). A topography of relationship disengagement and dissolution. In S. W. Duck (Ed.), *Personal relationships 4: Dissolving personal relationships* (pp. 1-29). New York: Academic Press.

Duval, S., & Wicklund, R. A. (1972). *A theory of objective self-awareness.* New York: Academic Press.

Festinger, L. (1954). A theory of social comparison processes. *Human Relations, 5,* 117-140.

Fishbein, M. J., & Laird, J. D. (1979). Concealment and disclosure: Some effects of information control on the person who controls. *Journal of Experimental Social Psychology, 15,* 114-121.

Fleming, R., Baum, A., Gisriel, M. M., & Gatchel, R. J. (1982). Mediating influences of social support at Three Mile Island. *Journal of Human Stress, 8*(3), 14-22.

Freud, S. (1904/1954). *The origins of psychoanalysis.* New York: Basic Books.

Gilbert, S. J. (1977). Effects of unanticipated self-disclosure on recipients of varying levels of self-esteem: A research note. *Human Communication Research, 3,* 368-371.

Gottlieb, B. H., & Wagner, F. (1991). Stress and social support in close relationships. In J. Ekhenrode (Ed.), *The social context of coping* (pp. 165-188). New York: Plenum.

Gottman, J. M. (1979). *Marital interaction: Experimental investigations.* New York: Academic Press.

Gottman, J. M., & Krokoff, L. J. (1989). Marital interaction and satisfaction: A longitudinal view. *Journal of Consulting and Clinical Psychology, 57,* 47-52.

Gottman, J. M., & Porterfield, A. L. (1981). Communicative competence in the nonverbal behavior of married couples. *Journal of Marriage and the Family, 43,* 817-824.

Green, S. K., & Sandos, P. (1983). Perceptions of male and female initiations of relationships. *Sex Roles, 9,* 849-852.

Grice, H. P. (1975). Logic and conversation. In P. Cole & J. L. Morgan (Eds.), *Syntax and semantics: Vol. 3. Speech acts* (pp. 41-58). New York: Seminar.

Harvey, J. H., Weber, A. L., & Orbuch, T. L. (1990). *Interpersonal accounts: A social psychological perspective.* Cambridge, MA: Basil Blackwell.

Hays, R. B. (1985). A longitudinal study of friendship development. *Journal of Personality and Social Psychology, 48,* 909-924.

Hazan, C., & Shaver, P. (1987). Romantic love conceptualized as an attachment process. *Journal of Personality and Social Psychology, 52,* 511-524.

Hendrick, S. S. (1981). Self-disclosure and marital satisfaction. *Journal of Personality and Social Psychology, 40,* 1150-1159.

Hendrick, S. S., Hendrick, C., & Adler, N. L. (1988). Romantic relationships: Love, satisfaction, and staying together. *Journal of Personality and Social Psychology, 54,* 980-988.

Henley, N. M., & Kramarae, C. (1991). Gender, power, and miscommunication. In N. Coupland, H. Giles, and J. M. Wiemann (Eds.), *"Miscommunication" and problematic talk* (pp. 18-43). Newbury Park, CA: Sage.

Hill, C. T., & Stull, D. E. (1987). Gender and self-disclosure: Strategies for exploring the issues. In V. J. Derlega & J. H. Berg (Eds.), *Self-disclosure: Theory, research, and therapy* (pp. 81-100). New York: Plenum.

Hobfoll, S. E., & London, P. (1986). The relationship of self-concept and social support to emotional distress among women during war. *Journal of Social and Clinical Psychology, 4,* 189-203.

Holtgraves, T. (1990). The language of self-disclosure. In H. Giles & W. P. Robinson (Eds.), *Handbook of language and social psychology* (pp. 191-207). Chichester, UK: John Wiley.

Horowitz, M. J. (1976). *Stress response syndromes.* New York: Jason Aronson.

Huston, T. L., & Ashmore, R. D. (1986). Women and men in personal relationships. In R. D. Ashmore & F. K. Del Boca (Eds.), *The social psychology of female-male relations: A critical analysis of central topics* (pp. 167-209). New York: Academic Press.

Huston, T. L., McHale, S. M., & Crouter, A. C. (1986). When the honeymoon's over: Changes in the marriage relationship over the first year. In R. Gilmour & S. Duck (Eds.), *The emerging science of personal relationships* (pp. 109-132). Hillsdale, NJ: Lawrence Erlbaum.

Jacobson, N. S., Waldron, H., & Moore, D. (1980). Toward a behavioral profile of marital distress. *Journal of Consulting and Clinical Psychology, 48,* 696-703.

Jones, D. C. (1991). Friendship satisfaction and gender: An examination of sex differences in contributors to friendship satisfaction. *Journal of Social and Personal Relationships, 8,* 167-185.

Jones, E. E., & Gordon, E. M. (1972). Timing of self-disclosure and its effects on personal attraction. *Journal of Personality and Social Psychology, 24,* 358-365.

Jourard, S. M. (1971a). *Self-disclosure: An experimental analysis of the transparent self.* New York: Wiley-Interscience.

Jourard, S. M. (1971b). *The transparent self* (2nd ed.). New York: Van Nostrand Reinhold.

Karpel, M. A. (1980). Family secrets: I. Conceptual and ethical issues in the relational context; II. Ethical and practical considerations in therapeutic management. *Family Process, 19,* 295-306.

Kelvin, P. (1977). Predictability, power and vulnerability in interpersonal attraction. In S. Duck (Ed.), *Theory and practice in interpersonal attraction* (pp. 355-378). New York: Academic Press.

Kessler, R. C., McLeod, J. D., & Wetherington, E. C. (1985). The costs of caring: A perspective on the relationship between sex and psychological distress. In I. G. Sarason & B. R. Sarason (Eds.), *Social support: Theory, research and application* (pp. 491-506). The Hague: Martinus Nijhog.

Knapp, M. (1984). *Interpersonal communication in human relationships.* Boston: Allyn & Bacon.

Knapp, M. L., & Vangelisti, A. L. (1991). *Interpersonal communication and human relationships* (2nd ed.). Boston: Allyn & Bacon.

Kobak, R. R., & Hazan, C. (1991). Attachment in marriage: Effects of security and accuracy of working models. *Journal of Personality and Social Psychology, 60,* 861-869.

La Gaipa, J. J. (1982). Rules and rituals in disengaging from relationships. In S. W. Duck (Ed.), *Personal relationships 4: Dissolving personal relationships* (pp. 189-210). New York: Academic Press.

Larson, D. G., & Chastain, R. L. (1990). Self-concealment: Conceptualization, measurement, and health implications. *Journal of Social and Clinical Psychology, 9,* 439-455.

Lehman, D. R., Ellard, J. H., & Wortman, C. B. (1986). Social support for the bereaved: Recipients' and providers' perspectives on what is helpful. *Journal of Consulting and Clinical Psychology, 54,* 438-446.

Levinger, G. (1983). Development and change. In H. H. Kelley, E. Berscheid, A. Christensen, J. H. Harvey, R. L. Huston, G. Levinger, E. McClintock, L. A. Peplau, & D. R. Peterson (Eds.), *Close relationships* (pp. 315-359). San Francisco: Freeman.

Levinger, G., & Breedlove, J. (1966). Interpersonal attraction and agreement. *Journal of Personality and Social Psychology, 3,* 367-372.

Levinger, G., & Senn, D. (1967). Disclosure of feelings in marriage. *Merrill-Palmer Quarterly, 13,* 237-249.

Levinger, G., & Snoek, D. J. (1972). *Attraction in relationship: A new look at interpersonal attraction.* Morristown, NJ: General Learning.

Lowenthal, M. F., & Haven, C. (1986). Interaction and adaptation: Intimacy as a critical variable. *American Sociological Review, 33*, 20-30.

Maccoby, E. E. (1990). Gender and relationships: A developmental account. *American Psychologist, 45,* 513-520.

Maccoby, E. E. (1991). Gender segregation in the workplace: Continuities and discontinuities from childhood to adulthood. In M. Frankenhauser, U. Lundberg, & M. Chesney (Eds.), *Women, work, and health* (pp. 3-16). New York: Plenum.

Maltz, D. N., & Borker, R. A. (1982). A cultural approach to male-female miscommunication. In J. J. Gumperz (Ed.), *Language and social identity* (pp. 195-216). Cambridge, UK: Cambridge University Press.

Markman, H. J., & Kraft, S. A. (1989). Men and women in marriage: Dealing with gender differences in marital therapy. *Behavior Therapist, 12*(3), 51-56.

McAdams, D. P. (1984). Human motives and personal relationships. In V. J. Derlega (Ed.), *Communication, intimacy, and close relationships* (pp. 41-70). Orlando, FL: Academic Press.

McCornack, S. A., & Parks, M. R. (1986). Deception detection and relationship development: The other side of trust. In M. L. McLaughlin (Ed.), *Communication yearbook 9* (pp. 377-389). Beverly Hills, CA: Sage.

Meichenbaum, D. (1977). *Cognitive behavior modification.* New York: Plenum.

Merton, R. K. (1948). The self-fulfilling prophecy. *Antioch Review, 8,* 193-210.

Metts, S. (1989). An exploratory investigation of deception in close relationships. *Journal of Social and Personal Relationships, 6,* 159-179.

Miell, D., & Duck, S. (1986). Strategies in developing friendships. In V. J. Derlega & B. A. Winstead (Eds.), *Friendship and social interaction* (pp. 129-143). New York: Springer Verlag.

Mikulincer, M., & Nachshon, O. (1991). Attachment styles and patterns of self-disclosure. *Journal of Personality and Social Psychology, 61,* 321-331.

Miller, G. R., Mongeau, P. A., & Sleight, C. (1986). Fudging with friends and lying to lovers: Deceptive communication in personal relationships. *Journal of Social and Personal Relationships, 3,* 495-512.

Miller, L. C. (1990). Intimacy and liking: Mutual influence and the role of unique relationships. *Journal of Personality and Social Psychology, 59,* 50-60.

Miller, L. C., & Berg, J. H. (1984). Selectivity and urgency in interpersonal exchange. In V. J. Derlega (Ed.), *Communication, intimacy, and close relationships* (pp. 161-205). Orlando, FL: Academic Press.

Miller, L. C., Berg, J. H., & Archer, R. L. (1983). Openers: Individuals who elicit intimate self-disclosure. *Journal of Personality and Social Psychology, 44,* 1234-1244.

Miller, L. C., & Read, S. J. (1987). Why am I telling you this? Self-disclosure in a goal-based model of personality. In V. J. Derlega & J. H. Berg (Eds.), *Self-disclosure: Theory, research, and therapy* (pp. 35-58). New York: Plenum.

Miller, R. S., & Lefcourt, H. M. (1983). Social intimacy: An important moderator of stressful life events. *American Journal of Community Psychology, 11,* 127-139.

Minuchin, S. (1974). *Families and family therapy.* Cambridge, MA: Harvard University Press.

Moffat, M. J., & Painter, C. (Eds.). (1974). *Revelations: Diaries of women.* New York: Vintage.

Montgomery, B. M. (1981). Verbal immediacy as a behavioral indicator of open communication content. *Communication Quarterly, 30,* 28-34.

Montgomery, B. M. (1984). Communication in intimate relationships: A research challenge. *Communication Quarterly, 32,* 318-323.

Morton, T. L. (1976). *Two-dimensional intimacy scoring system: Training manual.* Unpublished manuscript, University of Utah, Salt Lake City.

Morton, T. L. (1978). Intimacy and reciprocity of exchange: A comparison of spouses and strangers. *Journal of Personality and Social Psychology, 36,* 72-81.

Neale, J. M., Cox, D. S., Valdimarsdottir, H., & Stone, A. A. (1988). The relation between immunity and health: Comment on Pennebaker, Kiecolt-Glaser, and Glaser. *Journal of Consulting and Clinical Psychology, 56,* 636-637.

Newman, H. (1981). Communication with ongoing intimate relationships: An attributional perspective. *Personality and Social Psychology Bulletin, 7,* 59-70.

Notarius, C. I., & Johnson, J. (1982). Emotional expression in husbands and wives. *Journal of Marriage and the Family, 44,* 483-489.

Notarius, C. I., & Pellegrini, D. S. (1987). Differences between husbands and wives: Implications for understanding marital discord. In K. Hahlweg & M. J. Goldstein (Eds.), *Understanding major mental disorder: The contribution of family interaction research* (pp. 231-249). New York: Family Process.

Parks, M. (1982). Ideology in interpersonal communication: Off the couch and into the world. In M. Burgoon (Ed.), *Communication yearbook 5* (pp. 79-108). New Brunswick, NJ: Transaction Books.

Patterson, M. L. (1990). Functions of non-verbal behavior in social interaction. In H. Giles & W. P. Robinson (Eds.), *Handbook of language and social psychology* (pp. 101-120). Chichester, UK: John Wiley

Pennebaker, J. W. (1989). Confession, inhibition, and disease. In L. Berkowitz (Ed.), *Advances in experimental social psychology* (Vol. 22, pp. 211-244). New York: Academic Press.

Pennebaker, J. W., & Beall, S. (1986). Cognitive, emotional, and physiological components of confiding: Behavioral inhibition and disease. *Journal of Abnormal Psychology, 95,* 274-281.

Pennebaker, J. W., Colder, M., & Sharp, L. K. (1988). Accelerating the coping process. *Journal of Personality and Social Psychology, 58,* 528-537.

Pennebaker, J. W., & Hoover, C. W. (1985). Inhibition and cognition: Toward an understanding of trauma and disease. In R. J. Davidson, G. E. Schwartz, and D. Shapiro (Eds.), *Consciousness and self-regulation* (Vol. 4, pp. 107-136). New York: Plenum.

Pennebaker, J. W., Hughes, C. F., & O'Heeron, R. C. (1987). The psychophysiology of confession: Linking inhibitory and psychosomatic processes. *Journal of Personality and Social Psychology, 52,* 781-793.

Pennebaker, J. W., Kiecolt-Glaser, J. K., & Glaser, R. (1988a). Confronting traumatic experience and immunocompetence: A reply to Neale, Cox, Valdimarsdottir, and Stone. *Journal of Consulting and Clinical Psychology, 56,* 638-639.

Pennebaker, J. W., Kiecolt-Glaser, J. K., & Glaser, R. (1988b). Disclosure of traumas and immune function: Health implications of psychotherapy. *Journal of Consulting and Clinical Psychology, 56,* 239-245.

Pennebaker, J. W., & O'Heeron, R. C. (1984). Confiding in others and illness rate among spouses of suicide and accidental death victims. *Journal of Abnormal Psychology, 93,* 473-476.

Pennebaker, J. W., & Susman, J. R. (1988). Disclosure of traumas and psychosomatic processes. *Social Science and Medicine, 26,* 327-332.

Peplau, L., Rubin, Z., & Hill, C. (1977). Sexual intimacy in dating relationships. *Journal of Social Issues, 33*(2), 86-109.

Peters-Golden, H. (1982). Breast cancer: Varied perceptions of social support in the illness experience. *Social Science and Medicine, 16,* 483-491.

Petronio, S. (1991). Communication boundary management: A theoretical model of managing disclosure of private information between marital couples. *Communication Theory, 1,* 311-335.

Petronio, S., & Bantz, C. (in press). Controlling the ramifications of disclosure: "Don't tell anybody but . . . ." *Journal of Language and Social Psychology.*

Petronio, S., & Martin, J. N. (1986). Ramifications of revealing private information: A gender gap. *Journal of Clinical Psychology, 42,* 499-506.

Pilkington, C. J., & Richardson, D. R. (1988). Perceptions of risk in intimacy. *Journal of Social and Personal Relationships, 5,* 503-508.

Rawlins, W. K. (1983). Openness as problematic in ongoing friendships. Two conversational dilemmas. *Communication Monographs, 50,* 1-13.

Reis, H. T. (1990). The role of intimacy in interpersonal relations. *Journal of Social and Clinical Psychology, 9,* 15-30.

Reis, H. T., Senchak, M., & Solomon, B. (1985). Sex differences in the intimacy of social interaction: Further examination of potential explanations. *Journal of Personality and Social Psychology, 48,* 1204-1217.

Reis, H. T., & Shaver, P. (1988). Intimacy as an interpersonal process. In S. W. Duck (Ed.), *Handbook of personal relationships* (pp. 367-389). Chichester, UK: John Wiley.

Rogers, C. R. (1970). *Carl Rogers on encounter groups.* New York: Harper & Row.

Rohrbaugh, M., & Peterson, F. (1986, April). *The primary dyad in black and white families with normal and problem teenagers.* Paper presented at the Annual Meeting of the Eastern Psychological Association, New York.

Rosenblatt, P., & Meyer, C. (1986). Imagined interactions and the family. *Family Relations, 35,* 319-324.

Rosenfeld, L. B., & Bowen, G. L. (1991). Marital disclosure and marital satisfaction: Direct-effect versus interaction-effect models. *Western Journal of Speech Communication, 55,* 69-84.

Rosenfeld, L. B., & Kendrick, W. L. (1984). Choosing to open: An empirical investigation of subjective reasons for self-disclosing. *Western Journal of Speech Communication, 48,* 326-343.

Rosenfeld, L. B., & Welsh, S. M. (1985). Differences in self-disclosure in dual-career and single-career marriages. *Communication Monographs, 52,* 253-263.

Rubin, Z., Hill, C. T., Peplau, L. A., & Dunkel-Schetter, C. (1980). Self-disclosure in dating couples: Sex roles and the ethic of openness. *Journal of Marriage and the Family, 42,* 305-317.

Sarason, I. G., Sarason, B. R., & Pierce, G. R. (1990). Social support: The search for theory. *Journal of Social and Clinical Psychology, 9,* 133-147.

Schlenker, B. R. (1984). Identities, identifications, and relationships. In V. J. Derlega (Ed.), *Communication, intimacy, and close relationships* (pp. 71-104). Orlando, FL: Academic Press.

Selye, H. (1976). *The stress of life.* New York: McGraw-Hill.

Shapiro, A., & Swensen, C. H. (1969). Patterns of self-disclosure among married couples. *Journal of Counseling Psychology, 16,* 179-180.

Shaver, P., Hazan, C., & Bradshaw, D. (1988). Love as attachment: The integration of three behavioral systems. In R. J. Sternberg & M. L. Barnes (Eds.), *The psychology of love* (pp. 68-99). New Haven, CT: Yale University Press.

Shimanoff, S. B. (1987). Types of emotional disclosures and request compliance between spouses. *Communication Monographs, 54,* 85-100.

Silver, R. L., Boon, C., & Stones, M. H. (1983). Searching for meaning in misfortune: Making sense of incest. *Journal of Social Issues, 39*(2), 81-102.

Silver, R. L., & Wortman, C. B. (1980). Coping with undesirable life events. In J. Garber & M. E. P. Seligman (Eds.), *Human helplessness: Theory and applications* (pp. 279-375). New York: Academic Press.

Simmel, G. (1950). *The sociology of Georg Simmel* (K. H. Wolff, trans.) New York: Free Press.

Snell, W. E., Jr. (1986). The masculine role inventory: Components and correlates. *Sex Roles, 15,* 443-455.

Snell, W. E., Jr., Miller, R. S., & Belk, S. S. (1988). Development of the emotional self-disclosure scale. *Sex Roles, 18,* 59-73.

Snyder, M., Tanke, E. D., & Berscheid, E. (1977). Social perception and interpersonal behavior: On the self-fulfilling nature of social stereotypes. *Journal of Personality and Social Psychology, 35,* 656-666.

Spanier, G. B. (1976). Measuring dyadic adjustment: New scales for assessing the quality of marriage and similar dyads. *Journal of Marriage and the Family, 38*, 15-38.

Stiles, W. B. (1987). "I have to talk to somebody": A fever model of disclosure. In V. J. Derlega & J. H. Berg (Eds.), *Self-disclosure: Theory, research, and therapy* (pp. 257-282). New York: Plenum.

Stokes, J. P. (1983). Predicting satisfaction with social support from social network structure. *American Journal of Community Psychology, 11*, 141-152.

Stuhlmann, G. (Ed.). (1966). *The diary of Anais Nin, 1931-1934.* New York: Harcourt Brace Jovanovich.

Tannen, D. (1986). *That's not what I mean! How conversational style makes or breaks relationships.* New York: Ballantine.

Tannen, D. (1990). *You just don't understand: Women and men in conversation.* New York: Ballantine.

Tardy, C., Hosman, L., & Bradac, J. (1981). Disclosing self to friends and family: A reexamination of initial questions. *Communication Quarterly, 29*, 263-268.

Taylor, D. A., & Altman, I. (1966a). *Intimacy-scaled stimuli for use in research on interpersonal exchange* (Technical Report No. 9, MF 022.01.03-1002). Bethesda, MD: Naval Medical Research Institute.

Taylor, D. A., & Altman, I. (1966b). Intimacy-scaled stimuli for use in studies of interpersonal relations. *Psychological Reports, 19*, 729-730.

Taylor, D. A., Gould, R., & Brounstein, P. (1981). Effects of personalistic self-disclosure. *Personality and Social Psychology Bulletin, 7*, 487-492.

Taylor, S. E., Falke, R. L., Mazel, R. M., & Hilsberg, B. L. (1988). Sources of satisfaction and dissatisfaction among members of cancer support groups. In B. H. Gottlieb (Ed.), *Marshaling social support: Formats, processes, and effects* (pp. 187-208). Newbury Park, CA: Sage.

Thompson, E. H., Jr., & Pleck, J. H. (1987). The structure of male role norms. In M. S. Kimmel (Ed.), *Changing men: New directions in research on men and masculinity* (pp. 25-36). Newbury Park, CA: Sage.

Tolhuizen, J. H. (1986). Perceived communication indicators of evolutionary change in friendship. *Southern Communication Journal, 52*, 69-91.

Tolstedt, B. E., & Stokes, J. P. (1984). Self-disclosure, intimacy and the depenetration process. *Journal of Personality and Social Psychology, 46*, 84-90.

Vangelisti, A. (1991). *Family secrets: Forms, functions and correlates.* Unpublished manuscript, University of Texas, Austin.

Vangelisti, A. L., Knapp, M. L., & Daly, J. A. (1990). Conversational narcissism. *Communication Monographs, 57*, 251-274.

Waring, E. M. (1979). *The Waring Intimacy Questionnaire (Form 90).* Kingston, Canada: Author.

Waring, E. M. (1987). Self-disclosure in cognitive marital therapy. In V. J. Derlega & J. H. Berg (Eds.), *Self-disclosure: Theory, research, and therapy* (pp. 283-301). New York: Plenum.

Waring, E. M., & Chelune, G. J. (1983). Marital intimacy and self-disclosure. *Journal of Clinical Psychology, 39,* 183-190.

Waring, E. M., McElrath, D., Mitchell, P., & Derry, M. E. (1981). Intimacy and emotional illness in the general population. *Canadian Journal of Psychiatry, 26,* 167-172.

Waring, E. M., Tillmann, M. P., Frelick, L., Russell, L., & Weisz, G. (1980). Concepts of intimacy in the general population. *Journal of Nervous and Mental Disease, 168,* 471-474.

Wegner, D. M., Schneider, D. J., Carter III, S. R., & White, T. L. (1987). Paradoxical effects of thought suppression. *Journal of Personality and Social Psychology, 53,* 5-13.

Weiss, R. S. (1985). Men and the family. *Family Process, 24,* 49-58.

Weiss, R. S. (1990). Bringing work stress home. In J. Eckenrode & S. Gore (Eds.), *Stress between work and family* (pp. 17-37). New York: Plenum.

Westin, A. (1967). *Privacy and freedom.* New York: Atheneum.

Wheeler, L., Reis, H., & Nezlek, J. (1983). Loneliness, social interaction, and sex roles. *Journal of Personality and Social Psychology, 45,* 943-953.

Wills, T. A. (1981). Downward comparison principles in social psychology. *Psychological Bulletin, 90,* 245-271.

Wills, T. A. (1985). Supportive functions of interpersonal relationships. In S. Cohen & S. L. Syme (Eds.), *Social support and health* (pp. 61-82). New York: Academic Press.

Wills, T. A. (1990). Multiple networks and substance use. *Journal of Social and Clinical Psychology, 9,* 78-90.

Winston, B. V. (1992, April 9). I have AIDS. *Virginian-Pilot,* pp. A1-A2.

Wortman, C. B., & Conway, T. L. (1985). The role of social support in adaptation and recovery from physical illness. In S. Cohen & S. L. Syme (Eds.), *Social support and health* (pp. 281-301). New York: Academic Press.

Young, J. E. (1982). Loneliness, depression and cognitive therapy: Theory and application. In L. A. Peplau & D. Perlman (Eds.), *Loneliness* (pp. 379-405). New York: John Wiley.

Youniss, J., & Smollar, J. (1985). *Adolescent relations with mothers, fathers, and friends.* Chicago: University of Chicago Press.

Index

About the Authors

Valerian J. Derlega received his Ph.D. in social psychology from the University of Maryland in 1971. He is Professor of Psychology at Old Dominion University, Norfolk, Virginia. He recently co-authored the book *Psychotherapy as a Personal Relationship* and co-edited *Personality: Contemporary Theory and Research*. His research interests include self-disclosure, personal relationships, gender roles, and coping with stress. He presently is conducting studies on the effects of interpersonal touch on stress coping and on how the psychotherapy relationship is similar to other personal relationships.

Stephen T. Margulis received his Ph.D. in social psychology from the University of Minnesota in 1967. He is Professor of Facilities Management in the F. E. Seidman School of Business at Grand Valley State University, Grand Valley, Michigan. His research interests include social psychology, environmental psychology, facilities management, organizational behavior, and privacy regulation. He recently co-authored the two-volume work *Using Office Design to Increase Productivity*. He has been active professionally in the International Facility Management Association and in the Environmental Design Research Association.

Sandra Metts received her Ph.D. in communication research from the University of Iowa, Iowa City, in 1983 and has been teaching since that time in the Department of Communication at Illinois State University, Normal. Her research interests include the management of embarrassing episodes, relationship disengagement, deception in close relationships, and sexual communication. She has long been interested in how concern for social "face" influences the unfolding of problematic or awkward situations. Her work appears in a variety of journals, including *Communication Monographs, Human Communication Research,* and *Journal of Social and Personal Relationships,* as well as in edited volumes such as *Handbook of Interpersonal Communication, Studying Interpersonal Interaction, Sexuality in Close Relationships,* and *Close Relationship Loss: Theoretical Perspectives.*

Sandra Petronio has been Associate Professor in the Department of Communication at Arizona State University, Tempe, for the last 7 years. She received her BA from the State University of New York at Stony Brook in interdisciplinary social science, her MA in 1977 from the University of Michigan in social psychology, and her Ph.D. in 1979 also from the University of Michigan in communication. She has published research on aspects of informational privacy, disclosure, and embarrassment. She also has conducted research on gender issues, interpersonal relationships, and divorce adjustment.